Get Your Community Moving

ALA Editions purchases fund advocacy, awareness, and accreditation programs for library professionals worldwide.

Get Your Community Moving

Physical Literacy Programs for All Ages

JENN CARSON

CHICAGO 2018

Jenn Carson is a professional yoga teacher and the director of the L.P. Fisher Public Library in Woodstock, New Brunswick, Canada. She is the creator of the website www.yogainthelibrary.com and has been delivering movement-based programs in schools, libraries, and museums for a decade. She is currently obsessed with stand-up paddle-boarding, aerial yoga, and Brazilian Jiu Jitsu. Carson has a master's degree in library and information science from Drexel University. You can find her blogging about her physical literacy adventures at the ALA's Programming Librarian website (www.programminglibrarian.org).

© 2018 by the American Library Association

Extensive effort has gone into ensuring the reliability of the information in this book; however, the publisher makes no warranty, express or implied, with respect to the material contained herein.

ISBN: 978-0-8389-1725-1 (paper)

Library of Congress Cataloging in Publication Control Number: 2018003533

Cover design by Krista Joy Johnson.
Text design and composition by Karen Sheets de Gracia in the Mrs Eaves XL, Caecilia, and Omnes typefaces.

♾ This paper meets the requirements of ANSI/NISO Z39.48–1992 (Permanence of Paper).

Printed in the United States of America

22 21 20 19 18   5 4 3 2 1

This book is dedicated *to every tireless*
programming librarian
or paraprofessional who shows up
(often in costume and carrying supplies stolen from home)
and kicks ass—despite being overworked, underpaid,
short-staffed, and overwhelmed.
I see you. I am you. You are my people.

CONTENTS

Dr. Noah Lenstra

Here, finally, is the guidebook for how to serve the whole patron, the mind and the body together. Along with a hearty dose of inspirational wisdom, *Get Your Community Moving: Physical Literacy Programs for All Ages* contains tried-and-tested advice for how to infuse movement into your library. Read this book to learn what works and to become inspired to try something new. Jenn Carson should know—she has been working on this topic for over a decade.

Throughout her career, Jenn has graciously shared everything she has learned about how and why to move in libraries. I first met her after voraciously reading everything she had written in her blog on the ALA's "Programming Librarian" website and on her own "Yoga in the Library" website. I am not the only Jenn Carson junkie who eagerly awaits hearing about whatever new and inspiring programs she has developed as the director of the L.P. Fisher Public Library in the small town of Woodstock, New Brunswick. I have lost count of all the movement-based programs she does there, but I know they include everything from Brazilian Jiu Jitsu to snowshoes.

I find three things especially inspiring in Jenn's work. First, she weaves movement into all aspects of her library. Through things like stretch and move breaks for her adult knitting group and dance breaks for storytimes, Jenn's library offers endless opportunities to move and to be active together with others. Second, she has an unending passion for the health and wellness of library staff. Through her writing, speaking, and instruction, Jenn has inspired library workers throughout the United States and Canada to try new things and to have confidence in themselves as they move. Third, Jenn is fearless. She constantly works on new partnerships in her community to bring new forms of movement into her library and to take her library out to new groups (such as a local running club).

My decision to start researching movement-based programs in libraries emerged as a direct result of Jenn's writings. In the course of my research, I have found libraries all over the world that encourage movement among people of all ages and abilities, including libraries in Namibia, Romania, France, China, Singapore, Australia, and Brazil.[1] I have talked with hundreds of librarians who, through diverse programs and services, get people moving in their libraries. Nevertheless, I have found no one who has done as much on this topic for as long as Jenn Carson. This book distills her expertise into the practical advice that librarians of all types need to encourage and enable their patrons' healthy physical activity.

Why should we encourage movement in libraries? During my research I ask this question all the time. I think the best way to answer it is to turn to data. I asked 1,662 U.S. and Canadian public librarians in a spring 2017 survey why they have movement-based programs at their libraries. One librarian said, "It is stimulating to get up and move." Another said, "We like to offer our patrons something new to keep them coming back for more," A third said they "wanted to address the idea that the library is for the mind and the body." And one simply said, "for fun!"

Regardless of why libraries encourage movement, the data show that these programs work. Nearly 90 percent of the public libraries surveyed said that their movement-based programs had brought new users into their libraries, and 80 percent said the programs contributed to building their community. By portraying the library in a new way, movement-based programs bring new people into libraries and contribute to community self-care. A sizable percentage of respondents also said their movement-based programs contribute to literacy. Learning to move the body and learning to read are interconnected in many libraries, especially in services for very young children. This book addresses that topic, but it also shows how to develop programs that emphasize how literacy and movement are interconnected for people of *all* ages.

How should we encourage movement in libraries? Turn the pages of this book and find out! This book has all the answers: it should sit prominently on the shelf of any librarian who is interested in programs that work. I encourage librarians of all types to discuss this book during staff development days, at conferences, and online. Join the conversation and join the movement. It's time to move!

Note

1. For more information on the topics discussed in this foreword, please consult www.LetsMoveLibraries .org/physical-literacy-forward.

ACKNOWLEDGMENTS

This book could have never been written without the unending enthusiasm and support of the New Brunswick Public Library Service and its staff. For years you have been saying "Yes!" to my crazy, out-of-the-box, boundary-pushing ideas and letting me run with them. You've supported me when I've traveled to spread my physical literacy agenda at conferences and training days; you've let me publicly discuss what did and didn't work in our programs; and you've trusted me with increasingly complex levels of responsibility. Our patrons deserve a thank-you too, because we couldn't have tested out these programs without their willingness to show up for the outlandish, the unconventional, the sometimes downright physically demanding classes I dreamed up. The same goes for all of the community partners that provided money, supplies, and volunteer hours and who came with open hearts and minds. Major high-fives.

Many of the program ideas and obsessive ramblings offered in this book first became public through my blog on the ALA's "Programming Librarian" website. Sarah Ostman and her team at the website have been giving my voice a platform for the last three years, and she introduced me to Jamie Santoro at ALA Editions, who was excited to hear about physical literacy, asked me all sorts of questions, and offered me a book deal. Magic is real. Read on if you don't believe me.

One day, out of the blue, Dr. Noah Lenstra from the University of North Carolina (at Greensboro) contacted me and asked if he could call me to have a chat about the work I was doing creating movement-based programs. He said he had been teaching his students at the university about my efforts and wanted to connect with me because he was interested in starting a research project on the topic. I was not only humbled and touched that he had reached out, I was excited—someone else cared about this stuff too?! That first conversation led to a partnership which has created multiple surveys, websites, webinars, conference presentations, journal articles, and so much more. To have a colleague thousands of miles away give you so much support, brainstorm with you over the phone, collaborate on projects, write you letters of reference, edit your work, and do it all with the enthusiasm of a seven-year-old who is opening presents on Christmas morning, is a gift I can never show enough gratitude for. Noah sees the hard work we're doing out in the field to get people moving, and he wants to document it and celebrate it—and that, my friends, is a beautiful, precious thing.

One of the reasons why I decided to pursue my MSLIS degree at Drexel University was because of Dr. Denise Agosto. I wanted to pursue a concentration in youth services, and she is one of the foremost researchers and advocates in that area. I wasn't disappointed, since her classes were some of the highlights of my time there. But I gained additional respect for her when I asked her if she would be willing to supervise an independent project I was proposing: developing an online resource for kinesthetic programming. I had already been delivering movement-based programs in libraries, schools, and museums for years, but there seemed to be little or no research on the topic, and no practical guides for librarians to follow. Denise met my enthusiasm with a resounding "Go for it!" and so my website www.yogainthelibrary.com was born. I'm thrilled that she agreed to write the "Afterword" for this book.

This section could not be complete without a loud shout-out to Brendan Helmuth. He is the graphic genius who has tirelessly worked behind the scenes on all my posters, infographics, videos, and photographs. Ebony Scott, and her husband Craig, are also the photographers of many of the shots in this book. Without them to document what we're doing at the library, there would be no visual legacy to share with my readers.

Lastly, I must thank my family—my parents who supported me through this project by watching my children while I worked, and who fed me the world's best apple pie—and my kids themselves, Benjamin and Oliver. Without having you, my heart might never have broken open where it needed to in order to get me out of myself and into the world, where I belong. You are the bookends of my days—everything starts and ends with you.

A Moving Movement

Regarding your own childlike nature and play, does your job enliven you, pique your curiosity, fill you with excitement, challenge you, force you to take risks, make you laugh and cry? Do the people in your life ask you to play, to be a paradigm pioneer looking at things freshly and always open? Do you open others to all they can be, challenging them to take risks to accomplish their dreams?

—*Carla Hannaford*

It's a sunny Saturday in late March in my busy, small-town library in Woodstock, New Brunswick, Canada (population 5,254). At first, there's nothing terribly out of the ordinary about the scene: a short line at the circulation desk while staff attend to patrons; people sitting comfortably in the lobby sipping from paper coffee cups and reading the newspapers; someone scrolling through social media news feeds on a public access computer; and the noise of a book cart with a squeaky wheel being pushed on the second floor. But look more closely and you will see something else going on, something that is happening at more and more libraries all over Canada and the United States. There is a movement afoot, quite literally (pun gleefully intended). If you peer through the windows of my director's office, you'll notice I have a standing workstation for my desktop, an exercise ball I sit on for meetings, a pile of homemade beanbags on the bookshelf next to books about yoga and ergonomics, and way too many sneakers on a boot tray. You'll also notice that I'm not in the office.

If you peer into the multipurpose activity room next to the lobby of my library, at various times during the day or week, you may find a belly dance class happening, or a Frisbee demonstration, or a talk about healthy digestion, natural sleep remedies, or a local acupuncturist placing needles into a volunteer. You might even see our Run Club lacing up to head out for a five-kilometer run. Today it happens to be Seedy Saturday and the annual launch of our

Seed Library (figure I.1), so the room is filled with happy gardeners sharing potluck food, exchanging saved seeds, and discussing the best methods for staking tomatoes; and all the while, their children or grandchildren are weaving in and out between their legs or are quietly nursing while held in their parents' arms. Despite the small size of our community, the Seed Library's membership is diverse. The patrons from the local Amish and Mennonite communities are distinguishable by their humble dress and horse-drawn carts in the parking lot. A number of family members from a land-share commune upriver, with dreadlocked hair and layers of loose, organic cotton clothing, are discussing the benefits of cross-pollination for corn and using human manure as fertilizer. Some recent immigrants, resplendent in their colorful headscarves, are asking about the length of our growing season, accompanied by an interpreter from the Multicultural Association next door. There is a lineup in front of the repurposed card catalog, where thousands of seeds were painstakingly sorted, labeled, and wrapped in homemade envelopes at our Seed Sorting Party last weekend, and people are now checking them out with

FIGURE I.1 Seed library

their library cards. They are getting all the seeds they need to start their back-yard crops, for free, from local sources; these seeds are mostly organic heir-looms that have been tested for germination and are known to do well in our locality's conditions.

Overhead there is the pounding of little feet in our children's department, where kids of all ages take turns using the hopscotch mat, standing at one of our activity stations, acting out dramas in the dress-up center, or putting on an impromptu puppet show. A few are playing hide and seek, crouching behind a giant wooden Wampum Belt sculpture (figure I.2) that was made by our local Woodstock First Nation teens and is proudly on display for the month of March. As you walk up the stairs, you'll hear the faintest strumming of an acoustic guitar as a local musician plucks out soothing tunes in our cen-tury-old, high-ceilinged gem of a nonfiction section. There twenty-five adults and a few older children have spread out yoga mats and are reaching their arms skyward, turning their faces up to the sun streaming through our ornate windows, and feeling their feet firmly planted on the ground in the tree pose.

You'll find me there in the middle of it, leading these members of my com-munity in the collective joy of moving our bodies, in the best way we can, with the tools that we have. We stretch and ache, groan and laugh. When we suffer, we suffer together. Our library has programs about planning for funerals, for healing from trauma, for dealing with mental illness, for breathing through the discomfort of living in which we sometimes find ourselves. I feel energized in my role and strong in my convictions, and I am newly armed with a recent Innovation Award for my library's physical literacy initiatives. Libraries are not just repositories for books, though we are very good at giving people the information they need; we are becoming centers for wellness, for teaching

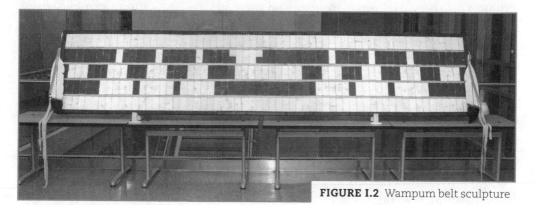

FIGURE I.2 Wampum belt sculpture

whole-person literacy, for a gathering of souls to stand together, embodied, and say, "This. This is community. Humans form tribes. We are social creatures. We need support and connection to feel at home in our bodies and minds. And I can get these needs met, for free, here, at my library, where everyone is welcome."

If you think my library, and my leadership, is unusual, I'm happy to gently reveal that you may soon have to admit you are wrong. According to Bertot et al., 23 percent of public libraries in the United States offered some sort of fitness program in 2013–2014.[1] In 2017 I helped Dr. Noah Lenstra, from the University of North Carolina (at Greensboro), design a survey which he administered to 1,662 librarians and other library staff members, and we began mapping the results.[2] To date, this map tracks hundreds of libraries across North America that are delivering movement-based programs in their communities, and it is the first comprehensive documentation of its kind on this topic.[3] From our collaboration and Dr. Lenstra's tireless data-collecting, I knew it wasn't just kinetics-obsessed me working away in isolation; there was a whole subset of librarians who were also fitness instructors or enthusiasts, and they were bringing their hobby to work and jumping on the wellness bandwagon that Loriene Roy championed while she was the ALA's president in 2007–2008. Many library staff suffer from chronic health conditions, stress-induced illness, and repetitive strain due to their jobs, and they are looking for ways to improve their own health. Throughout this book, the reader should follow the Activity All-Star sidebars to discover some of the amazing programs that are being created by pioneers in this field.

In order to get a good picture of what people were looking for in a programming book that could also serve as an introduction to physical literacy, I created a survey that was administered through the ALA's member newsletter. Of the more than 300 people who responded, 65 percent said their library offered some form of programming that encouraged physical activity.[4] The most popular offerings were yoga, dance, games, tai chi, martial arts, and gardening activities. The majority of respondents worked in public or school libraries. When asked to describe what impact these programs had on their patrons, many librarians were keen to describe how much fun the participants had and how the programs kept bringing them back to the library for more. Several respondents noted how meaningful it was to the members of their community with limited mobility that they offered chair yoga or exercise

Loriene Roy

Name: Loriene Roy, Professor

Contact: loriene@ischool.utexas.edu

Location: School of Information, University of Texas at Austin

Claim to Fame: Wellness Leader for the American Library Association

All-Star Program: ALA's Wellness Initiatives

When I was chosen to be president-elect of the American Library Association, I knew that this was an opportunity to not only serve libraries, but also to provide services and support for individual librarians. I had had a previous career as a medical imager, and my two undergraduate degrees were in allied health professions. I was greatly interested in how library workers might attend to their bodies so they could have great, active careers leading to great, active retirements. A group of colleagues formed my Presidential Advisory Circle, and they launched a workplace wellness initiative within the field and produced some useful resources. The group engaged in some useful discussions and helped plan a Wellness Fair that took place in the exhibit space of the ALA's Annual Conference in Anaheim in 2008. The Wellness Fair featured a chef demonstrating the preparation of health food, some information tables, and some exercise classes. The exercise classes were the most interesting and challenging to arrange. We had to work within a confined space, and we anticipated that our audience—the conference attendees—would be dressed in their daily professional wear. Thus, we arranged for librarians to provide the attendees with seated exercise classes: seated yoga, seated Pilates, and seated hula. We estimated that some 500 conference attendees visited the Wellness Fair.

In addition to the Wellness Fair, one of my former students, Henry Stokes, also designed a Workplace Wellness website. The content on the website included biographical wellness journeys and resources such as a guide to staying healthy at conferences. In 2016, a four-member group of ALA Emerging Leaders revisited the workplace wellness website and updated it.

After each ALA president's year, the ALA membership publication *American Libraries* devotes an issue to a topic related to the immediate past-president's focus. *American Libraries* chose the topic of wellness for the issue after my 2007–2008 term as the ALA president was over.

continued on the following page 》》》

⟨⟨⟨ continued from the previous page

Throughout the planning of the Wellness Fair, we were also in contact with the staff of the ALA-Allied Professional Association (ALA-APA). Due to a tax status different from that of the ALA, the ALA-APA can focus on the needs of the individual librarian such as salaries, unionization, certification, and workplace wellness. The ALA-APA conducted a survey of ALA members, inviting them to share details about how their workplaces supported their wellness. The ALA-APA reported the results of this survey in several articles in its newsletter, *Library Worklife*. I also launched a column on wellness in the newsletter. That column continues through the efforts of numerous contributors.

While I was able to highlight concern and interest in workplace wellness during my term as the ALA's president, I feel that this topic is only just beginning to gain traction in our professional networks. This slow adoption may be due to several factors. One is that librarians tend to focus on the services they provide for their patrons. Activities that address our own needs are not considered as important. We are also reluctant to share publicly our health concerns, yet each library worker I know can relate some personal story of weight loss, illness, or concern. And I had some pushback from library workers who felt I was promoting a certain body image that was not supportive of everyone; this was expressed by one librarian who wanted me to share the message that being overweight was also being healthy. I believe and have personally experienced that wellness is a topic whose interest only increases over time.

A spin-off of the workplace Wellness Fair and website was a subsequent workplace wellness symposium that I was able to host from November 2011 to May 2012. The symposium included a talk by Dr. Joanne Gard Marshall on locating wellness information. In addition, she demonstrated chair yoga. Analu Kame-eiamoku Josephides led the seated hula demonstration. Todd Whitthorne discussed preventive medicine, and staff from the South Central Region of the National Network of Libraries of Medicine provided training on the MedlinePlus.gov website. A representative of the Livestrong Foundation provided an overview of their resources. Dr. Barbara Bergin from Texas Orthopedics presented background on how to prevent and treat the maladies she sees among library workers.

This information has personally improved my quality of life. And I believe that other professionals could benefit greatly from learning about all of these topics related to workplace wellness.

classes. Many senior-focused programs were popular, with one librarian reporting that the age 50+ weekly exercise classes had made a notable impact on the balance, coordination, strength, and joint mobility of their partici-pants. Others said that library staff who participated in the programs subse-quently had fewer workplace injuries and were less stressed. One payoff that was mentioned was that physical literacy programs also boost libraries' circu-lation; for example, by playing CDs during class and making them available for checkout afterwards, and by highlighting the dance or children's CDs in the collection. Librarians were impressed by how offering free exercise pro-grams could get people into the library who might have otherwise never stepped through the doors, and these programs kept them coming back. In school libraries the programs often translated into an increase in reading by the students. The World Health Organization has stated that physical activity is an essential part of our lives and appears to be the *single most effective means* of influencing everyone's health and well-being.[5] I'll let you read that again so it can sink in. The number-one thing we can do to make everyone more healthy—healthy in a global, whole-person way—is to get them moving. Libraries and librarians are in the perfect position to offer movement-based programming, since we already have many of the skills and abilities needed, as Len Almond outlines in his essay "Physical Literacy and the Adult Population": "We need practitioners with the professional and educational skills to engage with people and help them to learn to love being active and care about their involvement. They need the skills to cultivate, nurture and help people to cherish their sense of vitality, energy and well-being, and avoid squandering the very essence of living."[6]

These are things most librarians engage in on a daily basis: nurturing, helping, teaching, and encouraging people to live better lives—from finding them resources on how to write a killer resume to distributing thousands of eclipse glasses so they don't burn their retinas. In other words, we do it all. Public librarians, especially, are the archetypal Jack and Jills of all trades. And I'm not the only librarian who is into sports and fitness; according to a 2010 survey, it's in the top five of librarian hobbies.[7] So offering movement-based programming is likely something you already do, maybe without even realiz-ing it, and I hope you are now thirsty to learn more.

When discussing the drawbacks to offering movement-based programs, besides the big three (time, space, money), the next hurdles that respondents to the survey indicated were lack of training, resources, or ideas of how to put a physical literacy program together. While I can't promise you more space or time, this book, and my websites (www.yogainthelibrary.com; www.jenncarson .com), will hopefully give you many practical program ideas that fit in your budget (or lack thereof). The curricula offered in this book have been organized by target audience, but many are adaptable to multiple demographic groups, and there are variations incorporated in each program model. There are also budget parameters, helpful tips, and ways to extend the program to increase circulation statistics and boost other literacies. I hope this book encourages you to engage with your patrons in a whole new way. And most especially, I hope it reminds you to take care of yourself. Because this world, depressing and chaotic as it can be, needs *you* to make it better. We librarians are a team of physical activity all-stars! It's time to get out there and start playing—let's go!

Notes

1. J. C. Bertot et al., "2014 Digital Inclusion Survey: Survey Findings and Results," University of Maryland, College Park: Information Policy & Access Center (iPAC), 2015, http://digitalinclusion.umd.edu/sites/ default/files/uploads/2014DigitalInclusionSurveyFinalRelease.pdf.

2. Noah Lenstra, e-mail message to author, August 29, 2017.

3. Noah Lenstra, "Map," Let's Move in Libraries, 2017, www.letsmovelibraries.org/map/.

4. Jenn Carson, "Physical Literacy: Movement-Based Programs in Libraries," survey, September 8, 2017.

5. World Health Organization, "The World Health Report—Conquering Suffering, Enriching Humanity," 1997, www.who.int/whr/1997/en/.

6. Len Almond, "Physical Literacy and the Older Adult Population," in *Physical Literacy throughout the Lifecourse*, ed. Margaret Whitehead (New York: Routledge, 2010), 125.

7. Stephen Abram, "Librarian Hobbies!! Here Are the Results," Stephen's Lighthouse: Illuminating Library Industry Trends, Innovation, and Information, 2010, http://stephenslighthouse.com/2010/10/31/ librarian-hobbies-here-are-the-results/.

What Is Physical Literacy and Why Does It Matter?

Before you've practiced, the theory is useless. After you've practiced, the theory is obvious.

—*David Williams*

Physical literacy. This term may be unfamiliar to you. I like to think of it as "bodily intelligence." A measurable intelligence, like cognitive or emotional intelligence, physical intelligence is being aware of our bodies and how they move in time and space. It is something we are born with and is shaped by our early environment, but it is also something that we can work to improve at any age. It is a skill, like empathy, or accounting. Physical literacy is defined by Margaret Whitehead, and the International Physical Literacy Association that she founded, as "the motivation, confidence, physical competence, knowledge and understanding to value and take responsibility for engagement in physical activities for life."[1] I would add that physical literacy is the motivation, ability, confidence, and understanding to move the body throughout the life course as *is appropriate to each person's capacity*. The development of fundamental movement skills that permit a person to move with confidence and control in a wide range of actions—such as throwing, skipping, or balancing—and environments, like on snow, grass, water, in the air or on ice—also applies to people with disabilities or exceptionalities. The throwing motion of someone in a wheelchair is going to look radically different from the throwing motion of someone who pitches for the big leagues.

Let's illustrate physical literacy by using two examples. A physically literate individual can read the surrounding environment and use that feedback to respond appropriately. In the first example, a child climbing a familiar tree adjusts his grip and foot placement based on the recent rains that made the branches more slippery than usual. He doesn't fall. If he does feel himself slipping, he readjusts his foot and hand placement. In the second example, a physically literate adult running on an unfamiliar trail adjusts her speed and watches the ground closely for roots and rocks and sudden changes in the terrain, minimizing her chance of injury. She notices when her thoughts distract her and she brings her focus back to the moment, her footfall, and the route ahead. These physically literate individuals don't need to be Olympic athletes or culturally sanctioned "perfect" physical specimens in order to have a high degree of bodily intelligence. The boy in our first example also happens to be blind in one eye. The woman running the trail is sixty-seven and is ten pounds overweight. They learn by doing, by practicing, by repeating these motions (climbing or running, respectively) in changing environments and adapting as their skills improve. This is called kinesthetic learning.

Babies and very young children cannot speak yet in a comprehensible language, but their babbling and chatter are the building blocks for later communication. The body must move when we communicate, even if it is only in subtle ways. Every culture on earth uses some form of hand gestures when speaking.[2] The first language we learn is nonverbal (physical); it's what we call *body language*, and it accounts for 50 percent of all human communication.[3] The combination of physical and verbal language creates a multisensory experience, triggering emotional and intellectual connections in the brain. Next time you want to tell a story, try sitting on your hands; you'll notice that this is not only very limiting and uncomfortable, but that other parts of your body (feet, head, elbows) will try to compensate by twitching and gesturing. Literacy (emotional, verbal, physical, financial, digital, etc.) is a whole-person experience that involves facial expressions (ever watch yourself in a mirror while you were doing a difficult math equation?), body gestures, intonation, touch, and feelings.

Human bodies are designed to move, and they begin to do so while we are still in the womb, as any pregnant woman can attest. Stimulating the vestibular system (which perceives body position and movement) through swinging, rolling, twirling, and cross-lateral movements in early life lowers a child's risk of later developing dyslexia and other learning disabilities.[4] According to Ratey and Hagerman (2008), for optimal brain development children should be physically active as often as possible because exercise is "the single most powerful tool to optimize brain function."[5] By mouthing objects, grasping with fingers and thumb, rolling over, lifting, waving, clapping, and eventually crawling and walking, babies are creating movement memory in their muscles, also known as *muscle memory*. Once our muscles have practiced a repetitive action (for better or worse), we can continue that action without conscious thought, like water that has worn away a groove in the rock and flows in the channel that it has created. The problem is, if we don't have high physical literacy skills, these channels (automatic actions) are often not the most effective way to get the water (body) where it needs to go, and in later life we end up with all kinds of disease, pain, and chronic conditions. As Kelly Starrett suggests in his revolutionary book *Deskbound: Standing Up to a Sitting World,* exercise is not enough.[6] We need to perform proper body maintenance (having good posture, breathing techniques, eating habits, etc.) so we can add to our health's bank account, because as we go through these daily, repetitive actions (driving a car, reaching for our phone, carrying a purse), which Starrett calls "duty cycles," we deplete the bank if we perform these tasks poorly.

Muscle memory is the internalizing of the movements we perform and experience.[7] We refine these movements until they become automatic. They become part of us. And thus we can only learn kinetically by *doing*. In fact, for the very youngest among us, without movement we won't even develop properly as humans. Our wrist joints, for example, are cartilaginous at birth and need lots of fine motor activity in order to strengthen, differentiate, and gain control.[8] In order for us to be able to hold a toothbrush properly, or a pencil (figure 1.1), we need to have practiced using those muscles—a lot. Most adults don't have to stop and think about how to brush their teeth, we just do it, but if you've ever helped a toddler get toothpaste on a toothbrush and into their mouth and then scrub their little teeth, you know very well that it is a learned skill which takes time and practice to acquire; it is not something that comes automatically, or can be learned easily from reading a book. There are consequences to being inactive and having poor technique: those kids who never learn to brush their teeth properly will end up with tooth decay and eventual digestive disorders; those who never learn to hold a pencil properly will have delays in learning how to read and write and will be inhibited in making art. Both tooth decay and low literacy rates affect self-esteem and quality of living in the long term, so this is serious business.

FIGURE 1.1 Pencil grip

Most children enter kindergarten as primarily kinesthetic or tactile learn-ers (in which they learn by physical activities), but by late elementary school most of them have transitioned to visual and auditory learning as their pri-mary method of acquiring information.[9] Kinesthetic learners learn best through doing and are most successful when totally engaged in an immersive experience, such as putting on a play, designing an art project, taking a field trip, exploring outdoors, or performing a science experiment.[10] Young chil-dren (aged five to eight) are still very much in the "here and now." Kenneth Fox, professor of health and exercise at Bristol University, has studied this age group, and finds that they are overly optimistic about their capabilities and don't have a strong grasp of how their abilities differ from their peers.[11] They believe top performers got that way because they were trying the hardest, and so you will see children this age putting in lots of effort, trying to please their parents and teachers, and getting easily frustrated when they can't "be the best." They are highly motivated but have short attention spans and little endurance. It is beyond the scope of this book to delve too deeply into child development, but there are many great resources listed in the bibliography. To really understand childhood from a physical literacy standpoint, you must read *A Moving Child Is a Learning Child: How the Body Teaches the Brain to Think* by Gill Connell and Cheryl McCarthy.

Children in the middle years (ages nine to twelve) become more accurate in their observations and start to understand that success comes from a com-bination of ability and effort, which begins to affect their motivation. They sometimes feel they don't have any talent for a certain physical activity, such as playing the drums or hitting home runs, and that their efforts aren't making a difference (which they often don't, in the short term). So they may give up with a shrug and say "Why bother?" This attitude, reinforced through experience (you simply *aren't* going to get any better at something if you don't practice) can persist into adolescence and eventually adulthood. By the time children become teens, establishing an identity among their peers becomes so important that they are unlikely to try something new and risk the ridicule and embarrassment of public displays of weakness or ineptness; instead, they adopt a posture of aloof detachment. This is why high-school gym teachers everywhere see a great divide between the sporty kids at the front of the pack competing for the finish line and those sauntering along at the edge of the track, who are just going through the motions. Those who are already skill-rich become richer and those who are skill-poor stay that way.[12]

Once people begin identifying themselves as strong or athletic, it tends to become self-reinforcing. Did you ever have a friend or coworker who decided to take up CrossFit or running, and all of a sudden their news feed becomes jammed with articles about their favorite sport, they make friends with similar obsessions, and they start wearing a lot more spandex and drinking protein shakes? Regardless of age, in order for our patrons to feel a sense of well-being and continued motivation, the following emotional needs must be met: a sense of competence (little improvements matter), a sense of autonomy (that's why forcing kids to participate in gym class rarely works), a sense of significance (the activity has to matter *to them*), and a sense of belonging (we're more likely to keep working toward our goals if we have shared that commitment with others).

Ed Ayres, the founder of *Running Times,* explores in his book *The Longest Race* how vitally important it is for us to maintain our physical fitness; our physical robustness is inextricably linked to our mental health, and without this acquired fortitude we will not have the inner fortitude or outer stamina we need to save the planet, which is our only long-term hope for survival. Ayres had an epiphany one day while reviewing his younger brother Alex's article in *Running Times* where Alex discusses how our circulatory and respiratory systems are responsible for oxygenating our muscles and our brain at the same time.[13] This was the moment when Ed Ayres realized that the body and mind are in fact *inseparable.* He goes on to discuss numerous studies that show a direct correlation between an increase in cardiovascular exercise and higher scores on tests of intelligence and concentration. He concludes that more oxygen to the muscles equals more oxygen to the brain, and this is more than just giving you a runner's high and an advantage on the court or in the boardroom; it gives you a more open heart and mind for learning and engagement.

Many of us in adulthood still learn very well kinesthetically. Many of our daily decisions—the ones we don't even consciously think about—and the tasks related to them use something called intuitive judgment, which was popularized in Malcolm Gladwell's bestseller *Blink*.[14] Intuitive judgment develops over time and is often gleaned from tacit knowledge. When we go about our day, interacting with different people, environments, and other information delivery systems, we are acquiring tacit knowledge, also known as "know-how." If you ask someone to explain in great detail how to go roller-blading for the first time, they would no doubt find the task of communicating that knowledge (without making any motion) difficult because it is so complex, and so rooted in the *doing*. It is much easier to show someone a complex task first, and then help them to try it themselves, rather than present the information in a more academic way.

Emotional self-regulation is another positive aspect of increased physical literacy. As Carla Hannaford says, you can't have an emotion without motion, so we should think of emotion as *energy-in-motion*.[15] Try it. I bet you can't express the emotion "happy" without at least a few muscles in your face moving. Margaret Whitehead concurs: "Movement or actions are the very material of emotion. Movement does not reveal an emotion; it is part and parcel of an emotion."[16] The study of how mirror neurons relate to empathy is fascinating, and unfortunately beyond the scope of this book, but I urge you to do some research of your own. It's been proven that those with higher levels of physical literacy (not just in one specific area—such as being a hockey star—but in a global, gestalt sense) can more readily sense what it's like to be in "someone else's shoes" and respond accordingly.[17]

We've seen above two examples of physically literate individuals in our tree climber and runner, so what might be an example of two people with low physical literacy skills? Everyone, even those with limited mobility, has some level of physical competence, but when we are addressing physical *illiteracy* we are observing (in ourselves and others) a lack of confidence or autonomy in approaching body-based activities. A young woman in excellent health has some friends who are going paddle-boarding at a nearby lake, but she doesn't know how to swim and is afraid to fall in the water. She doesn't want to admit that she never took swimming lessons because her parents couldn't afford it. She is embarrassed about needing to wear a life vest. The teen tells her friends she has to babysit her little sister and so she stays home, watching TV instead.

In another example, a middle-aged Native American man is interested in learning about yoga with the hope that it will relieve his chronic low-back pain. But he doesn't feel comfortable joining a yoga class at his local studio because he's been led to believe by marketing campaigns and social media that yoga is only for young, fit white women. He finds a few videos of African American men doing yoga on YouTube, but they are doing difficult poses with their huge, muscled limbs. He decides yoga isn't for him after all, and he takes some medication from the doctor to relieve his discomfort. Both of these individuals lack physical literacy skills.

Margaret Whitehead, in her seminal book *Physical Literacy throughout the Lifecourse*, maintains that physical literacy must be employed to take us beyond a "subsistence level." Here's her take on it:

> Physically illiterate individuals will avoid any involvement in physical activity in all situations wherever alternatives are possible. This could include not walking short distances, avoiding tasks such as house cleaning and gardening, preferring quick methods of preparing a meal and always using the remote control to turn on an electrical appliance. Individuals will not be motivated to take part in structured physical activity and will therefore not achieve refinement or development of their physical competence. They will have no confidence in their ability in the field of physical activity, anticipating no rewarding feedback from such involvement. Individuals will have a very low level of self-esteem with respect to this aspect of their potential and will avoid all inessential physical activity in order to guard against failure and humiliation.[18]

Sound familiar? I bet you know at least one person who fits this description, and you probably know many more than that. You might even be cringing a little at recognizing yourself in the description. In fact, even if we don't consider ourselves particularly sedentary, I bet there are certain activities we all avoid because we feel a lack of competence or are afraid of embarrassment. I, for one, spent most of my childhood avoiding the monkey bars in the playground due to my lack of upper body strength, and I was humiliated the few times I tried them; I fell, once even landing flat on my back and knocking the wind out of myself while some kids looked on and laughed. I might have even landed in a puddle. To this day, I'm ashamed of my lack of upper body strength and can barely do one chin-up. In order to improve my physical literacy in this area, I need to feel that I can achieve my goal of say, doing five chin-ups in a row, by practicing and noticing my progress in a safe, encouraging environment. I'm unlikely to go to a crowded gym and attempt to pull myself up on the bar in front of a bunch of experienced weight lifters. But if I had a bar in my own home, I might try it, though I might lack the motivation to keep doing it. A good solution might be to join a strength-training class for beginners with a supportive trainer where I could work on building this skill slowly, with others at a similar starting point.

You may look at pictures of me on the Internet doing aerial backbends while hanging from a hammock and think—*ok, that girl has some physical literacy skills right there*—but the truth of the matter is that pushing ourselves physically is something we can all benefit from, even (and perhaps especially) professional athletes. I coach a bunch of muscle-bound men at the local Brazilian Jiu Jitsu gym (figure 1.2) on how to use yoga to improve their flexibility, breathing, and mental state while competing, because all of their strength training has shortened their muscles, making them prone to injury and limiting their range of motion while delivering their deadly technique. This is why cross-training is so important for everyone, athletes or otherwise; it exposes your body to a wide range of experiences, and thus you can avoid overspecialization. We want the muscles to adapt, the neurons to wire and fire, in as many ways as possible. This gives us more options of how to respond appropriately and creatively in changing and challenging environments, whether we're being choked on the mats or just navigating a slippery sidewalk in a snowstorm. As Ed Ayres points out in his meditation on exercise and longevity: "To avoid stumbles, whether momentary or monumental, was not just an autonomic physical balancing act, but a critical skill at connecting the mindful present with the remembered past and the anticipated future."[19]

We don't have to be ultramarathoners like Ed Ayres, and thirty minutes of exercise is only 2 percent of a person's day, but many people still feel they don't have enough time to exercise, even though they spend many hours sitting in front of televisions or computer screens. How do we educate our

FIGURE 1.2 Brazilian Jiu Jitsu

patrons that physical activity needs to be a priority? The number-one reason why most people collapse on the couch at the end of the day is because they are exhausted. The last thing they feel like doing is putting on a pair of running shoes and heading out the door. But the magic of exercise is that it actually gives us *more* energy.[20] It comes down to physics and the law of perpetual motion vs. the law of inertia. An object that is already in motion will continue to stay in motion, and an object that is at rest will stay at rest, unless propelled into motion. We have to find a way to gain momentum to get ourselves up and moving. One way to do this is by starting physical activity early in the day. If we want our patrons to stay moving all day, it helps to offer physical literacy classes first thing in the morning. This won't work for everyone's schedules, but it is a good option. The next chapter will discuss how to implement these programs in your community, and each program model in the subsequent chapters has detailed descriptions to help you figure out how to make it work with your budget, time constraints, and skill set.

I hope you are starting to realize why it is so important for librarians teaching literacy to be aware of how physical literacy impacts our daily tasks—for both patrons and ourselves. In library work, unlike the kinesiology lab, it isn't all that important where we fall along the vast range of motion possibilities; what is important is learning how to push to our edge, and beyond, based on our unique capabilities. These embodied abilities may express themselves creatively, with whole-body action, such as dancing to our favorite song while we vacuum the children's department, or through fine motor skills such as cutting out craft props, or playing the piano during the annual Christmas concert. These physical capacities, as they develop, tie into our ability to achieve other literacies, such as holding a pencil, which allows us to form letters, which then allows us to write our stories. Physical literacy is just one component of what I call the gestalt, or "whole-person literacy." In order to be our best selves, we have to be given the opportunity and take the responsibility to develop each of our many literacies: emotional, digital, visual, physical, textual, financial, informational, verbal, auditory, cultural, numerical, environmental, and so on. Whitehead backs me up here when she says: "Because of the way physical literacy contributes to a wide range of other human attributes, such as language, cognition and rationality, the individual can grow in global self-confidence and self-esteem."[21] Our role, as facilitators of programs that encourage physical literacy, is to create a safe and welcoming environment where everyone is supported and encouraged to grow their skill set at their own pace. We're not here to make comparisons between participants; we're here to help them have fun enjoying their bodies, not as ornaments, or moving storehouses for our brains, but as evolving, fascinating instruments. Take a look at the infographic in figure 1.3 that shows the different components of physical literacy and how they can be improved at any age, and then turn the page to chapter 2 of this book so we can get started figuring out how to make this happen in your library![22]

PHYSICAL LITERACY

LEARNING BODY-BASED SKILLS IN CHILDHOOD CONTRIBUTES TO WHOLE-PERSON LITERACY THROUGHOUT THE LIFECOURSE.

By pushing physical boundaries, taking risks, and finding their edge, children wire their brains to **feel more comfortable with uncertainty**. This gives them the courage, as adults, to try new things, the perseverance to try again when it gets hard, and the confidence to make decisions, modify choices, and adapt in order to reach goals.

www.yogainthelibrary.com
www.programminglibrarian.org
www.physicalliteracyinthelibrary.com

Three of the most important skills for school-readiness (and work-readiness in adults) are the ability to **sit still, stay focused, and pay attention**. The vestibular system controls these, as well as posture and balance. Kids (and adults) usually fidget because they are trying to concentrate. Vestibular maturity (balance, stillness, orientation, concentration) is learned through movement.

Movement-based play helps children to develop spatial abilities, strength management, and **body awareness** (proprioception). This helps with everything from handwriting to playing sports, and not falling out of bed when we sleep!

Children develop **temporal awareness** (understanding timing) by moving through life's daily rhythms, developing body awareness, and learning to predict outcomes (what happens to the ball when I roll it?) This leads to the ability to analyze environmental data and make predictions in adulthood.

The power to use your body to complete tasks begins in early childhood, when **muscles develop as they are needed** in response to movement. Strength, stamina, flexibility, and agility are all acquired through active play.

It's never to late to hone your physical literacy

As a child improves their ability to move their body, their language and communication skills develop. Facial expressions, hand gestures, sound, and emotions make **communicating a whole-body process**. The more body-awareness you have, the better you can express yourself.

You can't have an emotion without motion. Feel happy and you smile. Feel frustrated and you tighten your muscles. **Emotions safely expressed through movement** (laughing, jumping, swaying, stomping, dancing, reaching out) allow children to practice experiencing multiple feelings at once, and identify, integrate and regulate them. This creates more emotionally mature adults who are better at empathizing with others.

Sources:

Connell, Gill, and Cheryl McCarthy. *A Moving Child Is a Learning Child: How the Body Teaches the Brain to Think (Birth to Age 7)*. Golden Valley, MN: Free Spirit, 2014.
Hannaford, Carla. *Playing in the Unified Field: Raising and Becoming Conscious, Creative Human Beings*. Salt Lake City, Utah: Great River Books, 2010.
Hannaford, Carla. *Smart Moves: Why Learning Is Not All in Your Head*. Arlington, VA: Great River Publishers, 1995.

Written and produced by Jenn Carson

FIGURE 1.3 Physical literacy infographic

Notes

1. International Physical Literacy Association, "Physical Literacy," 2016, https://www.physical-literacy.org.uk/.

2. Carla Hannaford, *Playing in the Unified Field: Raising & Becoming Conscious, Creative Human Beings* (Salt Lake City, UT: Great River Books, 2010).

3. Gill Connell and Cheryl McCarthy, *A Moving Child Is a Learning Child: How the Body Teaches the Brain to Think* (Grand Valley, MN: Free Spirit, 2014).

4. Hannaford, *Playing in the Unified Field*.

5. J. J. Ratey and E. Hagerman, *SPARK: The Revolutionary New Science of Exercise and the Brain* (New York: Little, Brown, 2008).

6. Kelly Starrett, Juliet Starrett, and Glen Cordoza, *Deskbound: Standing Up to a Sitting World* (Las Vegas, NV: Victory Belt, 2016).

7. Patricia Maude, "Physical Literacy and the Young Child," in *Physical Literacy throughout the Lifecourse*, ed. Margaret Whitehead (New York: Routledge, 2010), 107.

8. Ibid., 105.

9. Rita Dunn, Kenneth Dunn, and Janet Perrin, *Teaching Young Children through Their Individual Learning Styles: Practical Approaches for Grades K–2* (Toronto, ON: Pearson, 1994).

10. Angela Hanscom, *Balanced and Barefoot: How Unrestricted Outdoor Play Makes for Strong, Confident, and Capable Children* (Oakland, CA: New Harbinger, 2016).

11. Kenneth Fox, "The Physical Self and Physical Literacy," in *Physical Literacy throughout the Lifecourse*, ed. Margaret Whitehead (New York: Routledge, 2010), 74.

12. Ibid., 78.

13. Ed Ayres, *The Longest Race: A Lifelong Runner, an Iconic Ultramarathon, and the Case for Human Endurance* (New York: Experiment, 2012).

14. Malcolm Gladwell, *Blink: The Power of Thinking without Thinking* (New York: Little, Brown, 2005).

15. Carla Hannaford, *Smart Moves: Why Learning Is Not All in Your Head* (Salt Lake City, UT: Great River Books, 2005).

16. Margaret Whitehead, "Motivation and the Significance of Physical Literacy for Every Individual," in *Physical Literacy throughout the Lifecourse*, ed. Margaret Whitehead (New York: Routledge, 2010), 36.

17. Margaret Whitehead, "The Concept of Physical Literacy," in *Physical Literacy throughout the Lifecourse*, ed. Margaret Whitehead (New York: Routledge, 2010), 14.

18. Margaret Whitehead, "Introduction," in *Physical Literacy throughout the Lifecourse*, ed. Margaret Whitehead (New York: Routledge, 2010), 7.

19. Ayres, *The Longest Race*.

20. Len Almond, "Physical Literacy and the Older Adult Population," in *Physical Literacy throughout the Lifecourse*, ed. Margaret Whitehead (New York: Routledge, 2010), 120.

21. Whitehead, "The Concept of Physical Literacy," 13.

22. This infographic can be downloaded in a printable format at www.jenncarson.com/resources.html.

Getting Started

Implementing Movement-Based Programs in Your Library

Possibly the heart of our humanity is to want something we cannot achieve by our own efforts.

—Tim Farrington

The most overwhelming question when beginning anything new is "How do I start?" This is quickly followed by "What if it all goes wrong?" Well, I'm here to put you at ease, because we are going to walk through this together. The benefits of being a pioneer in a new field is that I've learned what works and what doesn't work. I've made lots of mistakes and lived through failures so you don't have to. Don't get me wrong: I have no magic programming wand I can wave and say "presto!" to deliver you a cranky patron-proof, prepackaged program with guaranteed results and statistics that will make your supervisor's jaw drop. But I *can* write you out a program model for things I have tried and tested, advising you on the following items: planning strategies, variations on the theme (so you can do it many times, many ways, if it works for you), materials required, how it will impact your bottom line, partnership opportunities, marketing, and ways to tie the new program in to what you are already doing and utilize the strengths of your team and collection. Like anything, the more you do it, the easier it will get, and the next thing you know you'll be finding all sorts of ways to include movement in many of your programs. But until then, let's do the hard work of strategizing how to make your first movement-based program successful, because anyone who's worked in library programming for more than two months knows that without a solid plan in place, your odds of an enjoyable experience are low (and your staff and possibly your patrons' experience might be even worse—yikes!).

Funding

Let's talk right off the bat about one of the hardest things—money. We'll get this subject out of the way so we can talk about the fun stuff later (like learning dance moves!). Not all of your movement-literacy programs are going to be easy on your budget. But the good news is that many of them will be. Or they will at least be workable with the right partners. If you are like me and run a midsized, small-town library with a modest program budget funded by the municipality, you probably need to make your dollars stretch as far as possible; this could mean resorting to rummaging around for toilet paper tubes and cardstock in your own recycling bin. I once joked to my staff that librarians and teachers are the only employees on the planet who steal from *home* to bring supplies to *work*, instead of the other way around. If, on the other hand, you have so much money left over in your program budget at the end of the year that you're scratching your head trying to come up with ideas to spend your money on, you can skip right to the next section and we'll try not to hate you too much.

The first two questions I ask when designing a new program are: Who is going to teach this program? What supplies do they need? The answers you come up with will determine your bottom line. First and foremost, always, *always* mine your staff for their hidden abilities, strengths, interests, and hobbies. Have you got a circulation clerk who likes to square dance on the weekend with his wife? See if they'd be interested in starting a square-dance club at the library (provided you have the space). Have you got a zealous board-game junkie lurking in the break room who is trying to get someone to play Spot It? Recruit him to run a life-sized Jenga or Twister tournament. Think waaaaay outside the box. Think beyond your immediate programming staff. Does your technical services guru like to run on her lunch break? See if she'd be willing to lead a 5-kilometer fun run, maybe on her own time if programming doesn't fit into her work plan. Ask the janitor if he's ever thought about coming in to demonstrate his black-belt karate moves during a martial-arts-themed storytime. So the first step here is to make *connections* with your staff. Discover who your allies are. You don't have to do this alone. Other people care about moving their bodies too. Find them, listen to their stories about their interests and hobbies, and then (gently) beg them to share their wisdom. You'll know when you've hit the jackpot, because they'll be as excited as you are.

After you've mined your staff for treasure, move on to your volunteers and patrons. See if they'd be willing to volunteer to teach a class or do a demonstration. I have a wonderful patron, Deborah Helle (figure 2.1), who teaches a belly dance *and* a ballroom dance program (she alternates every six weeks) for free, as a way to share her love of dance with the community. She is retired and her husband is no longer mobile enough to dance with her, so one of my male staffers graciously volunteered to be her assistant, and after more than a year of dancing together they are now pretty darn impressive swinging around our activity room. At the end of every six-week session, I buy Deborah a little thank-you (a gift card to a local restaurant or a bouquet of flowers). She doesn't expect it, but she keeps coming back, and I want her to know she's appreciated. A nice big bunch of flowers is still much cheaper than hiring an instructor, and by purchasing from the town florist or local family-owned restaurant the library is supporting local businesses.

What if you don't find anyone willing to donate their time to the library? A good place to start looking for instructors is on Facebook groups or at places where instructors might congregate. For example, if you are looking for a yoga teacher, you could join a local yoga interest group on Facebook; ask if there are any student-teachers looking for hours at your local yoga training studio (new teachers are required to have a certain number of hours in order to be certified); contact Yoga Alliance or another yoga association; or look in the local classifieds (online, in the paper, or on bulletin boards). For kids' programs, try contacting local child care centers for volunteers or finding government-

FIGURE 2.1 Jenn and Deborah

funded wellness programs you can piggyback on. For example, I partnered with our local early intervention service, which delivered many amazing pre-school readiness programs at our library, with a very low budget (under $200 for supplies)—see the Activity All-Star sidebar to learn more about one of these programs. Once you do find a willing facilitator, and you tell them it is for your library, they will usually offer a non-profit rate. I have a Celtic dance instructor who charges me $5 per child per session. Even if I get a roomful of kids, that's still less than $150.

Another budget-bolstering trick up the librarian's sleeve is to apply for grant funding. In the United States there is a National Coalition for Promoting Physical Activity. You can find a list of the members at www.ncppa.org/membership. Here in New Brunswick, the Western Valley Wellness Network regularly gives my library money to cover the cost of refreshments or facilitators for wellness-related programs. The Rotary Club or another local charity group can also be a good place to ask. A local food security network may be able to help you feed the folks. You can probably find local government or corporate-funded agencies that offer this sort of financing if you are willing to go digging and fill out the paperwork. You might also have a local business that would be happy to sponsor your event in exchange for a public acknowledgment. I have a local business owner whose wife and children are regular program attendees, and he will often enthusiastically make donations towards programming ideas I run by him. I get to run the programs and buy the materials I need, and his family has great programs to go to at the library. Win-win.

I recommend a think-outside-the-box approach to acquiring props and prizes. Instead of just working from a learned-helplessness approach (understandable in these days of dwindling or nonexistent program budgets) and throwing your hands up in the air, you should think hard about ways to modify your programs in order to meet your budget. Can't afford yoga blocks? Use thick, discarded books—I know you have those. Can't afford fancy massage balls? Use dog-toys or tennis balls from the local dollar store. Can't afford yoga mats? Do chair yoga—you probably have chairs. Can't afford healthy snacks? Ask a local farmer to donate bruised fruit or veggies he can't sell and cut them up yourself. I regularly acquire free merchandise (T-shirts, magnets, water bottles, etc.) from physical literacy nonprofits such as Active for Life and use them as prizes at events.[2] A *can-do* attitude can go a long way in overcoming perceived financial barriers. Admittedly, the results might not be perfect.

《《《 ACTIVITY ALL-STAR 》》》

Marilyn Cleal

Name: Marilyn Cleal, Family and Early Childhood Educator

Contact: 1–855–454–3762

Location: Woodstock, New Brunswick, Canada

Claim to Fame: Working for Family & Early Childhood West for seventeen years, focusing on multiple methods of learning—visual, auditory, tactile, and kinesthetic. Motto: Engagement is the name of the game.

All-Star Program: ABC Boom!

ABC Boom! is a program based on developmental progression and the theory that children's physical development progresses from the core out. Therefore, children cannot run before they can walk and children cannot print before they know shapes and strokes. The ABC Boom! program that we facilitate is eight sessions in length. The parents/caregivers come to the first session to receive an introduction and some theory on physical motor movement. Then the remaining seven sessions are dedicated to teaching the fourteen "strokes," two at each session. Parents attend the sessions with the children so they can follow up at home.

The program has a step-by-step method for teaching the strokes. Each of the strokes has a pictogram, a fun sound, and a physical activity associated with it. The first stroke that is taught is called "The Raindrop." The Raindrop makes the "plop" sound. There are added word blowouts to each of the large poster-size pictograms. The facilitator points out the blowouts and names them for the children. The children are then asked to say the word. Then the pictogram is presented on a chalkboard and the stroke is modeled for them. There are existing pictograms on the board, and only the stroke is completed while making the sound.

We use large physical movements so that the children can feel it with their whole body. For "The Raindrop" they are asked to stand on a stool and jump from the stool, pretending that they are raindrops while saying the "plop" sound. They also have another activity in which they hold a beanbag high in the air and let it drop while making the "plop" sound.

continued on the following page 》》》

continued from the previous page ❭❭❭

The child is then asked to trace or mark the stroke on the chalkboard using the "wet, dry, and try" in large markings about twenty-four inches high. The wet is using a damp sponge, the dry is using an eraser, and the try is using different colors of chalk. The repetition of the stroke in these different mediums helps cement the concept in the child's memory.

After this we ask the child to use their finger and imitate what is drawn in the air. Then the child is asked to make the stroke on their own in the air, and then the child is asked to do it with their eyes closed. Until the child is able to do this step with all of the strokes, it would not be developmentally appropriate to take it to paper. These three steps are repeated again, but this time using a ribbon stick.

At the end of each session we sing a song, to the tune of the "Wheels on the Bus," with one verse dedicated to each of the strokes. We sing two verses from the week before and add the two new verses.

The family is asked to brainstorm ways to use a laminated 8½ × 11-inch copy of the stroke that is sent home. One thing that it may be used for is a password. The child is also given a small memento of the stroke. For "The Raindrop" it is a beanbag. To further intertwine literacy with the children's physical development, we also have short children's books based on each of the strokes. The books provide opportunities within them to practice the strokes. The blowout words are also there for the parents to model.

ABC Boom! is a fun interactive program that engages children. The win-win is that parents have a way of supporting their children once they know the strokes to form letters, and many of our local schools are using ABC Boom! in their kindergarten classes. This gives children a heads-up. ABC Boom! also helps to prevent problems with letter reversal, letter direction, and handwriting speed.[1]

Your activity room might not look like a set from a glossy magazine or be popular on Pinterest. That's okay. Show up. Do the work. The patrons will have fun because you make it fun, not because you are blowing a wad of cash on them.

Partnerships

Sometimes the people or organizations you partner with, as mentioned above, can provide you with the monetary funds or materials you need to run your program successfully. The assistance they provide can be something simple; for example, you want to have a pumpkin-decorating program for Halloween and you already have lots of paint, glue, glitter, and feathers in your stash, but no pumpkins—and no money to buy them. But you can call a local farmer, grocer, market, or distributor to see if they will donate some pumpkins. One year we had a local organic farm donate twenty pie pumpkins that were too small to sell but were perfect for kids to decorate and take home! We put their logo on the Facebook event and gave them a big shout-out.

Sometimes you can establish deeper kinds of collaboration—people can provide you with their time, expertise, and enthusiasm, as well as funding—and you can provide them with exposure, a headquarters or meeting place, and an outlet for their passion or their agenda. Let me give you an example of one such partnership at work in my library.

I wanted to provide more mental health programming at my library, since it is a real need in my community (and in every community, I suspect), but I have little training in that area (other than a minor in psychology, some time spent briefly volunteering at a methadone clinic, and a few professional development workshops). The Canadian Mental Health Association (CMHA) does a great job raising awareness about mental health issues on a national scale, but I figured they might need some help getting their programs to the people who might actually need them in small communities. Here, on the public library front lines, we have an abundance of patrons who are in desperate need of some connection with these sorts of services. So I put the two together and first contacted our local Suicide Prevention Committee to plan an ASIST training (suicide first aid) in our library, free of charge to anyone who wanted to attend.[3] Then I connected with Lee Thomas from our local CHMA chapter, and we met and made a list of all the issues I felt were most pressing in my community, including addiction, LGBT support, grief counseling, eating disorders and body awareness issues, suicide prevention, caregiver support, and barriers to getting help.[4] We started drawing up an action plan for how we would tackle these needs over the next year: grief support meetings at the library, a peer-to-peer outreach program for teens, Yoga for Heart Ache, a monthly Body Image Bootcamp (for teens and adults; figure 2.2), awareness campaigns, and creating an LGBT library support group called the Chromatic Collective.[5] We would share the responsibilities; for example, Lee would source the funding to pay for food for a program, while I would request money from my library board to buy workbooks for participants. Lee would take care of the cognitive-behavioral therapy part of the presentation, while I would focus on the mindfulness or movement portion. Putting our skills and resources together allowed us to deliver programs to our patrons that we wouldn't have been able to access otherwise.

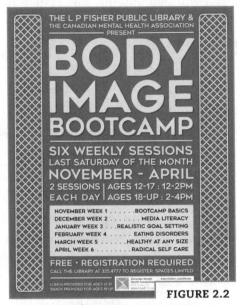

FIGURE 2.2

Body Image Bootcamp poster

This is just one example of how reaching out to create partnerships in your community can lead to innovative program development and delivery. I can tell you from experience that not every time will be successful, for myriad reasons, but I challenge you to keep trying, to keep reaching out. Try not to feel overwhelmed because you can't possibly deliver all of the programs you want to by yourself, because you don't need to—that's what positive partnerships are for. Make the connections and you'll be surprised and thrilled at all the wonderful places they will lead.

Legal Issues

There are a great many issues that will no doubt be brought up by concerned citizens, your administration, staff, board members, and any other stakeholders when you say you want to start offering movement-based programs. Let's unpack some of these sticky wickets so you are armed with the knowledge you need to support your advocacy for these services.

First, what about the issue of risky play? What if someone gets hurt? I'm about to get unpopular here, but I'm in good company. According to Angela Hanscom, author of *Balanced and Barefoot: How Unrestricted Outdoor Play Makes for Strong, Confident, and Capable Children,* taking physical risks teaches safety by practicing body awareness and building confidence.[6] Here are some examples of activities that provide a healthy amount of risk for (age-appropriate) children and which can be done during library programs with supervision:

spinning in circles, jumping off boxes/ledges, dancing, balancing, rolling down a hill (if you have one nearby), going upside down, tumbling/gymnastics/yoga classes, crawling, climbing, cutting with scissors, whittling with knives, and cooking. As children spin in circles, the utricles in their ears are activated and send messages to the brain about the orientation of the head. Activating the vestibular system promotes a feeling of grounding and focused presence.[7]

Dr. Peter Gray, author of *Free to Learn*, tells the story of a little boy who was deeply involved in a craft making Christmas ornaments. A nearby woman stopped Dr. Gray to express her concern that a five-year-old was being allowed to use a hot glue gun by himself. Gray assured the woman that he was watching from a distance to make sure the gun was being used responsibly, and he noted that the little boy, left to his own devices, was actually being exceedingly careful with the hot object. Gray reflects on the experience:

> There is no need to caution him or to do the gluing for him. The former would interrupt his concentration and the latter would spoil his play completely. I am grateful that the boy's parents and all others who see him are wise enough to leave him alone at this activity. Imagine all the ways that an over-involved adult could ruin his play. The adult could deprive him of the challenge by kindly doing all the difficult or "dangerous" parts for him, distract his concentration with unsolicited advice or cheerful chatter, hurry him along so he could get to other projects but have inadequate time for this one, or praise his work in ways that would shift his attention away from the process (which is most important to him) and toward the product (which is less important).[8]

This is what is known in libraries and schools as process-based learning instead of product-based learning. The end result of making the ornament (like hitting a target with an arrow) is much less important than creating the muscle memory involved in practicing something in our own time and space (like shooting the arrow over and over).

Let's use another craft example to illustrate this, since most public librarians are very familiar with making storytime crafts with children. Think about a time you made a snowman out of cotton balls (every winter for the last few years, right?). You can make a sample to show the group, give the kids the construction paper and glue, demonstrate how to put the big ball on the bottom, the medium-sized ball in the middle, and the small ball on top and then draw some arms and a hat. Everyone's artwork will look more or less the same at the end, depending on their skill and age. In fact, it will look an awful lot like the same snowman you made. There is nothing inherently wrong with product-based learning for teaching fundamental skills, like pattern recognition or awareness of colors and shapes. But it does little for artistic expression or for opening people up to that flow state where they are just drifting along, lost in a very restorative mind-space. Plus, it's a lot more work for you preparing all those little cut-outs ahead of time and giving those instructions over and over. Contrast this with giving the kids a bunch of construction paper, cotton balls, glue, and crayons and saying, "Let's make a winter scene! What are some things that remind you of winter?" And then letting the children come up with their ideas on their own, with very little nudging or input from you. At first some of them, used to product-based programming, may find this uncomfortable. They may want rules to follow. They may be afraid to take risks. Adults will have an even harder time with this ("What if I get hurt? What if I look foolish?"). Let them be bored. Let them get frustrated or overwhelmed. Let them take reasonable risks. (I think eight-year-olds can safely use low-heat glue guns as long as they show reasonable judgment, but I'll let you decide what you—or your policies—dictate.) The children will eventually participate, or else they will opt out, or they will copy what someone next to them is doing. That's okay. It is giving them space to try a new way of approaching the world, and this is a good thing. It gives them more tools in their toolbox.

At the end of the free play-style session you will have a whole bunch of interesting artwork. None of it may look like a stiff, stereotypical snowman made out of cotton balls, which generate very little to talk about or engage with afterward. Instead, with process-based learning you get to ask the children to share stories about their pieces, if they want. Listen to their stories. They will be fascinating! Watch their body language as they talk about their artwork and how they made it. Observe the improvements they make in their fine motor skills while they work. They get bonus points if they are standing at their workstations, shifting from foot to foot while they concentrate. Your job, as facilitator, is to get out of their way and let their bodies learn how they learn best: through discovering, moving, and feeling out their environment. Watch how this freedom of movement and thought directly enhances their sociability, their language skills, their tolerance for uncertainty, and especially their self-efficacy. Yes, there is the risk that someone will get hurt—a burn from a glue gun, a toothpick in the eye—but taking small, manageable risks is how we learn. This is physical literacy in action.

Now let's loop this back to a totally movement-based program, such as a water balloon fight (figure 2.3). How can you guarantee someone isn't going to get hurt if you just let kids "free play" and pelt each other with water balloons? Well, first, you can't. You cannot guarantee that everyone, everywhere, at any time will be 100 percent safe. If you wrapped the kids in cotton gauze before you play, no doubt someone would be allergic to cotton, or be claustrophobic and have a panic attack. Your job is to facilitate the safest program space possible while also leaving room for creativity—no easy task—and this is worth it for the joy it brings to your patrons. We must create healthy boundaries, including having a no-tolerance rule if someone breaks them. For example, every patron (or their legal guardian) participating in a movement program at your library needs to sign a liability form (also known as a "holds harmless" form).[9] If they don't sign, they don't play. Period. Next, there must be safety rules that everyone follows in order to participate. For example, no aiming water balloons above the neck. If someone breaks the rule, even once, they are out for the rest

FIGURE 2.3 Water balloon game

of the game. A safer example would be to not have a water balloon fight at all, and instead to throw balloons at nonhuman targets, some of which could be rigged to move so you get the same physical literacy benefits without the risks. You have to decide what you (and your staff and administration) can tolerate as a "reasonable" amount of risk. I will discuss these risk factors in each of the program models in this book and offer alternatives and helpful hints. Just remember, there is risk involved with inertia. Staying still and sedentary has just as many indications for injury as something like water skiing, and in fact some would argue it has even more, as we'll discuss throughout this book.

Another legal issue to consider is the qualifications and insurance coverage of your facilitators. Check with your building insurance, your employees' union (if they are unionized), worker's compensation board, and other legal and work-safe entities to see what your employees can and cannot do at work, and what they will be covered for if they get hurt or someone gets hurt under their watch. In my workplace, the staff are covered by our insurance if we get hurt on the job or if a patron gets hurt while attending a program. But this insurance *does not* cover volunteers or paid instructors coming into our facilities. Because of this, we often ask instructors to have personal liability insurance. Yoga teachers, for example, can register for this insurance with Yoga Alliance (for members) or other insurance companies.[10] If I have a substitute come in to cover one of my yoga classes, I require them to have proof of liability insurance. Check with your administration to see what your policies are on these matters (and if you don't have them, create them).

One last thing to think about is requiring criminal record checks, and background checks or references, for anyone working with vulnerable sectors of the population (children, the elderly, the disabled, etc.). Don't just take their word for it that they have a clean record; require that they show *recent* proof from your local or state/provincial law enforcement agency, and call all their references. Don't assume, just because it says on their resume they've worked with children or in a nursing home, that they have the skills and integrity required for the job. Do your homework.

Training

One question I regularly get asked is, "Do you need to be a yoga teacher to teach yoga at the library?" My first answer is always "Yes, but . . ." If you are going to provide full-on yoga programs, you need to either have someone on staff who is a certified yoga teacher with at least 200 hours of training, or you need to hire a teacher or recruit a volunteer from your community. If they are providing classes to patrons with special needs and many of the yoga poses or postures need to be modified, the teacher should also have some background in anatomy and should know how to make adjustments to the poses.

That said, do I think you need to be a fully certified yoga teacher when you just want to add a few fun poses to a children's storytime or add a little meditation break to your workday? No, absolutely not. As long as you've had at least six months' experience practicing yoga and meditation yourself, I don't see why you can't share that experience in a fun and safe way with others. Another alternative would be to bring in an experienced yoga instructor to teach your staff the basics so they feel more confident delivering yoga as part of their existing programs.

Everything I just said about yoga programs also applies to any other sort of fitness program. You want to have a legitimate tai chi master lead a class, not a volunteer who has just watched a few videos online. Send your staff (and yourself) to as many physical literacy trainings as you can afford. Last summer two of my staff came with me to take Superhero Training, which combined three different physical literacy workshops in one day (and was paid for by a grant I applied for).[11] On your own time you should learn as much as you can about the sports you are interested in. As a yoga teacher, I spend much of my vacation time away at yoga trainings. I have to pay for these myself, but they benefit the programs I deliver at the library and make me a happier person: win-win!

But that said, you don't need to be a trained Olympian to bust a move or two. Trust your own knowledge and don't be afraid to work a few movements into existing programs—I've been known to throw in a few belly-dancing moves to shake up a boring afternoon training session or shoot a Nerf Gun to blow off steam with my staff (and I have no right to either shimmy my hips in a qualified capacity or carry a weapon). Be professional, safe, and have fun too.

Patron Feedback

Ugh. I'm sorry. We do have to talk about this. People will complain, as you know. All the time. About everything. I recently had a patron complain that we were offering too many "physical programs" and not enough "lectures or book-related programs." I gently (okay, I was a *wee* bit defensive) reminded her that we had recently hosted a literary festival which included a writing workshop and book readings; we'd had a lecture by a retired senator on the future of democracy; we were home to five or six very active book clubs; and we'd had four or five book launches in the last few months. I also asked the patron what we could do to offer programming that would better meet her needs. We collaborated on some ideas, which I will follow through on. In other words, I listened. And then I made plans to the best of my abilities and resources to meet her needs.

No one patron in the library is more important than any other (despite what they may tell you), and it is our job to make sure we are meeting as many possible needs as we can with the skills, resources, space, and time we have, based on our organization's mission and strategic plan. That's why it is so important to elicit feedback from your patrons, and really listen to what they have to say. The ones with "strong opinions" will tell you everything they are thinking whether it is valuable information or not. Listen, smile, nod, take notes, and try not to get your back up. But you also really need to seek feedback from the ones who never say anything at all, and this is where evaluation forms at the end of a program can prove to be very helpful.[12] Hand them out at the end of a program, or else create a general survey to give out to your patrons, perhaps at your annual general meeting, asking them what programs they would like to see offered in the year ahead. And don't forget to also solicit the opinions of the marginalized and the illiterate, who may not attend your current programs, feel comfortable with paper or electronic forms, or engage socially with the staff; their thoughts about our services are important too.

One common complaint you will get is that libraries shouldn't be teaching movement-based programs, they should be places where people can read quietly. You will even get this complaint from staff and possibly your boss. Please hand them this book, or just photocopy the best bits. Or show them Noah Lenstra's map, as discussed previously, of the thousands of libraries in North America that are now offering physical literacy programs to much applause.[13]

Another issue that may come up is patrons (or staff and administration) insisting that yoga is a religion and therefore should not be taught in public institutions. The word *yoga* means "union," to yoke, to join together. Yoga is the joining of the mind and body to bring the whole person into harmony. It is an eight-limbed system designed to lead a person towards enlightenment, of which hatha yoga (or the physical poses) is only one component. The physical poses are designed to calm and focus the mind while preparing the body for long periods of contemplation and meditation. Yoga has been around for an estimated 5,000 years, but many of the poses we recognize, like sun salutations, have only been added over the last few centuries. Hatha yoga isn't a religion or a cult, so there are no worries about indoctrinating any of your patrons or students. Some people may still complain, but that's okay; you can't please everyone all of the time. I usually offer these people a book on yoga from our library.

Marketing

In each program model in this book, there will be a list of different ideas for how to market your program, including poster examples. You probably already know how to reach your audience best. At my library we use Facebook events and posts, our website, print posters, print calendars, word of mouth, press releases to news outlets, and occasional public service announcement call-ins to radio stations. We're working on an electronic newsletter, but we have to be careful of the delivery method due to the new anti-spam legislation in Canada.[14] You might also want to consider marketing through Twitter, Instagram, paid ads, or other outlets. In my rural community, Facebook, the website, a calendar, and posters on bulletin boards seem to work best.

Our library branch sends out most of its marketing material in English, even though New Brunswick is a bilingual province, because our region is primarily anglophone, but all of our event information is translated into French and English for the website, so there is always at least one multilingual source. Other library branches in the province send their materials out in both languages, or primarily in French. Think about your community, review its most recent census, and decide what languages would reach the most patrons—you can't translate everything, so pick your top two or three languages. In the United States these would be English and Spanish.

When I hire frontline staff I look to see what secondary skills they have, besides a good customer service/library background, and I ask them if they would be happy to use these skills in their new workplace. They always are. Because of this technique, I now have two professional photographers/

videographers and a graphic designer on staff. The benefits are that many of our events are beautifully captured, and a poster that I would spend six hours fiddling with in Microsoft Publisher and which would look absolutely horrendous is made in an hour in InDesign by my talented staff member. He gets to use his skills and we get a professionally designed poster.

Logistics

Each program model in this book will discuss the best time of day to host the event, as well as the space, staff/volunteers, and props required. When it comes to the topic of dress for physical literacy programs, we need to be culturally sensitive. Every region of the world has its own culturally sanctioned physical activities, such as different forms of dance, play, or competitive sports, as well as the uniforms worn for these specific forms. If you work in a culturally diverse library, you may have people who show up for a movement-based program wearing everything from short-shorts and tube tops to *hijabs*, saris, cowboy boots, track pants, or an Amish bonnet. Luckily, as Margaret Whitehead points out, the basic components of physical literacy are the same in every culture.[15] Throwing a ball overhand with accuracy and good form is the same in Texas as it is in Vietnam, and bicycles are ridden all over the world in the same fashion (albeit in many different conditions).

In Western culture, our everyday tasks rely more on fine motor coordination and small muscle groups, like those used to operate a smartphone or write a story. Unless you work on a farm or build houses, you are unlikely to repetitively engage large muscle groups or lift heavy things all day long. This is not the case in other parts of the world, where people do heavy manual labor and walk many miles a day. This is all the more reason for us to offer opportunities for movement in libraries. We are encouraging those who come from more active cultures to remain engaged and embodied with their physical selves and not adopt the sedentary lifestyle of most North Americans. And we are giving those raised in the West an opportunity to change unhealthy habits and learn new skills, while having fun and making friends.

Notes

1. ABC Boum! was originally designed in French by authors Natasha Rouleau and Josée Leblanc, of Quebec. Their website is http://abcboum.net/. To receive training in the English version of the program (ABC Boom!), visit http://otkidscan.com/.

2. Contact Active for Life for great physical literacy resources: http://activeforlife.com/.

3. For more information on ASIST training, visit https://www.livingworks.net/programs/asist/.

4. For more information on the work Lee Thomas does breaking down mental health barriers, visit https://www.leethomas.ca/.

5. I had started a similar group with the same name (chosen by the students) while I was working at the New Brunswick College of Craft and Design, and we decided to work from that same program model in Woodstock since it was so effective: space to talk, film clips, book recommendations, and advocacy, in other words, a safe, low-key space to connect.

6. Angela J. Hanscom, *Balanced and Barefoot: How Unrestricted Outdoor Play Makes for Strong, Confident, and Capable Children* (Oakland, CA: New Harbinger, 2016).

7. Mary J. Kwar and Ron Frick, *Astronaut Training: A Sound Activated Vestibular-Visual Protocol for Moving, Looking, and Listening* (Madison, WI: Vital Links, 2005).

8. Peter Gray, "How to Ruin Children's Play: Supervise, Praise, Intervene," *Psychology Today*, 2009, https://www.psychologytoday.com/blog/freedom-learn/200901/how-ruin-children-s-play-supervise-praise-intervene.

9. Here is a sample liability waiver from the New Brunswick Public Library Service: http://www2.gnb.ca/content/dam/gnb/Departments/nbpl-sbpnb/pdf/politiques-policies/1085_library-programs_appendix-a.pdf.

10. For an example, visit the Yoga Alliance at https://www.yogaalliance.org/AlliantInsurance.

11. To learn more about Superhero Training, please visit https://www.superhero-nb.ca/. I highly recommend it for all programming staff in public libraries.

12. Here's a sample evaluation form from the New Brunswick Public Library Service: http://www2.gnb.ca/content/dam/gnb/Departments/nbpl-sbpnb/pdf/politiques-policies/1085_library-programs_appendix-b.pdf.

13. If you forgot about it already, that's okay! Go here right now: www.letsmovelibraries.org/.

14. Government of Canada, "Canada's Law on Spam and Other Electronic Threats," Canada's Anti-Spam Legislation, 2017, http://fightspam.gc.ca/eic/site/030.nsf/eng/home.

15. Margaret Whitehead, "Motivation and the Significance of Physical Literacy for Every Individual," in *Physical Literacy throughout the Lifecourse*, ed. Margaret Whitehead (New York: Routledge, 2010), 41.

Passive Play

Sneaking Physical Literacy into Existing Spaces

A library is a miracle. A place where you can learn just about anything, for free. A place where your mind can come alive.

—*Josh Hanagarne*

If you've reached this chapter of the book, you may be starting to get sold on the idea that there really is something to the whole physical literacy business, or maybe you're already on the bandwagon. But some of you might be thinking: that's all well and good in *theory,* but how does she know it works in real life, in real libraries—in our messy, busy, complex world?

Back when I was a clerk, I cut my teeth introducing movement-based programs in libraries when I obtained my certification to teach children's yoga in 2009 and my indulgent, long-suffering director, Leslye McVicar, who rarely said "no" to my wild programming ideas, gave me permission to run with it. Children's yoga proved so successful and rewarding that I also used my 200-hour training to teach adults. And soon I was teaching yoga programs pretty regularly at the library and even in the park across the street. A number of families with kids on the autism spectrum would come to my programs, and I would adapt the format to help everyone participate. I started designing programs for kids with exceptionalities at a local occupational therapy clinic. I seemed to have a knack for using movement to reach kids who were sometimes challenging to communicate with, for those who didn't engage in the way that was expected of them, but who were capable of engaging nonetheless. I was learning from them. I was making mistakes. But I was figuring it out as I went along. I was happy and proud of the work I was doing.

And then my marriage fell apart. It happened brutally and unexpectedly. My ex-husband became unemployed. I suddenly found myself a single mother with a mortgage and car payments and mouths to feed, and I only had the salary of a part-time library clerk. So I took an additional job doing applied behavior analysis with children aged eighteen months to four years who had been diagnosed as being on the autism spectrum. We worked in tight quarters, I didn't agree with the punishment/reward aspects of the treatment, and I found myself desperate to connect with the kids in a more holistic way. We were trained to try to get them to sit still, focus on the task at hand, stop stimming (short for "self-stimulation": repetitive motions that help the person focus or self-soothe), and even make eye contact, if possible. I didn't see anything wrong with avoiding eye contact, which I often did myself when I felt withdrawn or unsafe. I found myself rushing through the lesson plans so I could take the kids outside for free play, or to jump on the mini-trampoline inside if it was raining. They seemed happiest and most themselves when moving, even if those movements simply involved hand-flapping, rocking, thumb-sucking, or repetitive eye-blinking. Someone with as much energy as me has spent much of her life fidgeting, or bouncing, or knitting, chewing, or playing with her hair in order to stay focused, so it didn't seem that abnormal. In fact, it kind of made sense.

A few years later, I left library work for a while and took a position as a behavioral interventionist in a middle school, working with children that had a range of issues that interfered with their ability to function in the classroom. This was when my intuitive, developing knowledge of physical literacy took over. I quickly discovered every behavior communicated a need. The kids I worked with had so many behavioral-emotional disorders that they just couldn't sit still in class, and their teachers didn't have the time or skills to work with them individually, so they would send them to me. Many of these kids were malnourished, neglected, highly dramatic, or extremely withdrawn; sometimes they were suicidal, they were often manipulative, and they could easily get violent (I've had more than one chair thrown in my classroom). I would often take them outside to collect litter, run laps, throw around a football, have a snack, do some yoga, or just pick up sticks and hit things. At first the teachers and administration were furious that I wasn't "punishing" the kids for "bad" behavior by making them do worksheets or having a "time-out," but they quickly saw the results I was getting. The kids were much more willing to settle into their work once they had gotten their "fidgets" out. My study of Dr. Carla Hannaford's work taught me that you can't have an emotion without motion, and these kids were full of all sorts of complicated emotions that needed to find a safe place to move out of their bodies. Soon I was asked to lead a group training on the topic for all the teaching assistants and other interventionists in our region, and I found myself teaching a modified yoga and meditation curriculum to the teachers so they could use it in their classrooms. Instead of focusing on controlling the behavior, I addressed the children's needs—for attention, a safe space to talk, physical activity, nutrition, etc.—and the behavior naturally improved.

Let me turn the moment over to you for a second, dear reader: where are you reading this right now? Are you in an environment or mood that is conducive to the absorbing task of taking in new information, or are your brain and body having to fight both intrusive internal and external stimuli in order to focus? Like the kids in my story, you may find it very difficult to concentrate if there is a lot going on in your emotional landscape: work deadlines looming, a family crisis, ill health, financial troubles, a fight with your significant other, or political upheaval in the news. And like the students in my intervention room, you may not have the right physical environment that lends itself to quiet contemplation or periods of study: a lack of healthy food, ill-fitting clothes, uncomfortable furniture, a noisy room (or a ringing phone and full in-box), the wrong prescription in your glasses (or no glasses at all when you need them), or even possible threats of violence or dismissal. Maybe you just really need a nap, or a hug, or a deep, deep breath. Maybe your way to cope with this unease is to fidget, chew gum, play Candy Crush on your phone, check Facebook, light a cigarette, eat a candy bar, put on some background music, or just simply close this book and decide you can't concentrate and maybe didn't want to read right now anyway.

Some people, those of us who are wired to be kinesthetic learners, can't help but move when we're absorbing information. Forcing us to sit still actually works against the way our minds absorb and process information. There's been a lot of research done, recently compiled in a book called *Rest: Why You Get More Done When You Work Less* by Alex Soojung-Kim Pang, about how important walking and other forms of exercise have been to some of the world's most important artists, thinkers, and scientists.[1] By engaging their bodies in the repetitive task of perpetual motion, these masters of thought freed up enough space in their mental landscape to come to their innovative and unique (and sometimes paradigm-shifting) conclusions. In his recent book *Deskbound: Standing Up to a Sitting World*, Kelly Starrett argues that sitting is killing us. My staff have an adjustable workstation for processing the mail, and our circulation desk has multiple levels. Our patrons also have a choice between standing and sitting workstations. Getting everyday tasks done, like completing time sheets, counting the bank deposit, or answering e-mails, seems to really work for me at a standing station. But when I want to do something more in-depth, something which requires a good chunk of time and concentration, like reading through a new twenty-page policy memo, or perusing a vendor catalog, or composing a blog post, I'll sit on my bouncy exercise ball, so I can pleasantly stim (wiggle and bounce) just enough to stay on task. I keep healthy snacks and water handy. I take stretch breaks. When I really, really need to think about something, I go for a long, solitary walk or run. In other words, I have learned, through much trial and error, to create an environment (and respond to it) in a way that allows me to function as efficiently and harmoniously as possible, given my conditioning and predisposition.

So the question then becomes: What are we doing in our libraries to create environments that meet the needs of all types of learners? How do we remove the obstacles to our patrons acquiring the literacy skills that we, as libraries, are committed to improving; these barriers can be things like hunger, safe space, health issues (mental and physical), time constraints, financial worries, and even just lack of access to resources such as the Internet, a printer, or a fitness class. I can hear you now, and I feel the same way myself: "But Jenn, we can't be everything to everyone, we can't possibly meet the complex and competing needs of all our patrons, all the time. We don't have the budget, the staffing, or the facilities. We don't have the time!" And your library may not allow certain programs. A rare book facility is unlikely to want to introduce a healthy snack bar; an academic library with a noise-level policy can't introduce a Zumba class in the stacks; a prison library can't give inmates golf clubs or Nerf blasters; and a cramped one-person, one-room rural library operating out of the town hall is unlikely to be able to pull off an all-day bike expo in the parking lot without an army of volunteers and the grace of a higher power. But what you can do is tweak the environment to give your users more options to enhance their physical literacy while taking part in your services. The rare book facility could offer a display of health and exercise-related materials for inspiration. The academic library could check out yoga mats or pedometers as an alternative collection, or install treadmill desks (if they were quiet enough, maybe in soundproof study rooms?). The prison library could offer meditation classes or a deck of mindfulness or yoga activity cards that patrons could take back to their cells. The rural, one-person library could install a small (perhaps portable) movement station so young visitors could be active while their parents looked through the stacks. And remember, you can always sneak some physical literacy into existing programs by giving people opportunities to move and stretch, by doing ice-breaker games that involve movement (more on this in the program models), or by adding a few yoga poses to a storytime. Here are some more passive program ideas to inspire you.

Alternatives to Sitting

If you haven't read Kelly Starrett's *Deskbound: Standing Up to a Sitting World* or bought a copy for your library, you should do that immediately. Right now. I'll wait.

I have been sitting on an exercise ball for over a decade as an alternative to an office chair, but it wasn't until I threw my back out in spring 2017 that I read Starrett's book and transitioned to a standing workstation, which I have been using ever since (and so far, no more back pain). I still have a regular office chair for fancy meetings (and my exercise ball chair for everything else), but 90 percent of my work is performed on my feet. At Dr. Starrett's suggestion, I also now include ten minutes a day of body maintenance work with a lacrosse ball I keep on my desk, in addition to some yoga stretches. It is beyond the scope of this book to get into the ergonomics of a healthy workstation, but I have a webinar I did for the ALA's Programming Librarian website that you can watch for free on YouTube.[2]

Like most health advice, it is best to use common sense when applying it in your own life. I don't stand still all day—I move around. And the reality is that some people just *can't* stand or walk due to mobility or chronic pain issues. Moreover, there is no guarantee that standing or moving around will boost alertness or performance. As Alex Pang explores in his book *Rest*, it is important that users set their own pace at treadmill desks, because it actually takes more attention to walk at a pace that is not your own natural gait. In fact, walking is better for subconscious mind-wandering, and letting your brain sift through complex data to arrive at novel solutions. Many artists and scientists have had their "eureka!" moments while out for a stroll. So treadmill desks aren't ideal for focused thinking or tasks that require attention to detail (such as balancing accounts), but they are great for other work. It sure is nice to offer the option of a treadmill desk, if you can afford it. There are a number of libraries, mostly academic, that now have treadmill or bike desks, and if you can afford one (or more), you should consider it. If not, make sure you have varied work spaces that give people the option to sit or stand. Another option is to put "fidget bars" under desks so kids and adults have a bar to put their foot on as they swing back and forth while they work—this can help kinesthetic learners to focus, and it helps everyone keep the blood pumping. You could also consider offering exercise balls instead of office chairs; just make sure to get the kind on a base with locking wheels so your patrons don't roll away![3]

Interactive Learning Spaces

According to the International Play Association, "playing is a process, not an activity."[4] As we saw in chapter 1, moving the body is essential for muscular growth and mental and physical well-being. Play, being freely chosen and self-directed (preferably without adult intervention), allows children the opportunity to enter a flow state, which is both deeply restorative and also energizing. By creating interactive learning spaces that children can approach in their own time and engage with in their own fashion, libraries give kids this much-needed opportunity for imaginative physical engagement (figure 3.1). There is a movement in China, started by Cheng Xueqin, called Anji Play, which encourages children aged 3–6 to be masters of their own environment. This program is even being adopted by public libraries and community centers in the United States.[5] I highly encourage you to read Cheng's Fundamental Rights of Play at www.anjiplay.com/rights. If you are still skeptical about the link between physical play and heightened literacy skills, just Google "literacy" and "block play." You may have heard of a similar movement in Germany with Forest Kindergartens. My own children's day care center here in Woodstock, New Brunswick, has an outdoor classroom that children spend a good part of the day in, no matter what the season. It is a magical place. If it is possible, consider adding an outdoor play space at your library. It doesn't have to be built of expensive, commercial playground equipment. It could be as simple as some bricks and blocks of wood on a lawn where children can create their own play environment. It doesn't even have to be a permanent installation; you could bring out oversized games, like a giant Connect Four board, bead table, or large wooden dominoes, and let the kids play with them during certain hours without planning a detailed program.

Another option, indoor or out, is to create a weaving wall. This is a vertical space where children (or adults) weave feathers, leaves, or other found-in-nature objects into twine, yarn, beaded strings, or fabric. Each time they visit the library they can add a new treasure to the wall. It can be a permanent installation or a one-time portable program. I'm currently having a large weaving wall built by a local woodworker with locking casters on the bottom so we can move it to different locations in the library. You can also purchase them commercially.[6] Google "nature weaving" to get some good ideas of small-scale models you can build yourself out of sticks.

Indoors, if you have the space, you can install climbing and play structures that target gross motor skills. If you don't have the space, you can buy a portable plastic slide like I did and leave it in your children's department, putting it

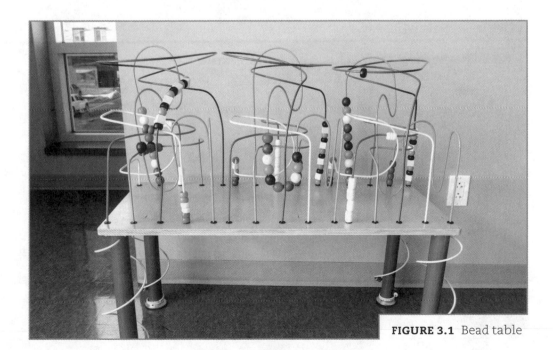

FIGURE 3.1 Bead table

FIGURE 3.2 Hopscotch

in storage when you need the space for something else. I also bought a hopscotch carpet (figure 3.2); it takes up hardly any space and it encourages the kids to play. A nearby basket of beanbags is good too.

Another indoor option for child-led physical play is setting up dramatic play centers, such as puppet theaters (figure 3.3), play kitchens, dress-up centers, sensory tables, stand-up maker counters, pretend flower shops, shoe stores, ice cream shops, veterinarian's offices, restaurants, mechanic's garages, grocery stores, and so on. We have a few of these spaces in our library and they are very popular. You can also install wall-mounted interactive stations where younger children can pull levers, press buttons, slide beads, and more. This keeps children engaged in a meaningful way while parents look for books to take home (or sometimes just stare at their phones). Another thing I like to do is leave activity cards out, such as a yoga deck, for children and their

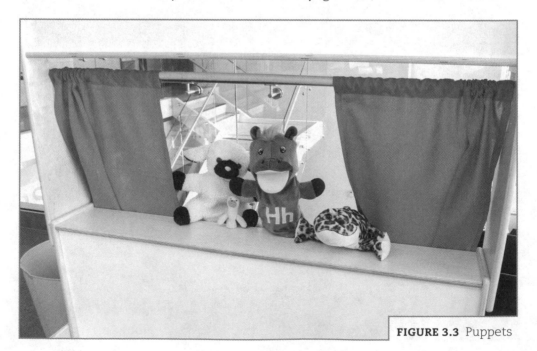

FIGURE 3.3 Puppets

caregivers to try out.[7] Yes, these cards will occasionally get bent, ripped, or stolen, but for the average price of about fifteen dollars it's totally worth it to see a mom or dad doing a tree pose with their kids on a Saturday morning.

Passive Activity Programming

Anytime you aren't actively leading a program, but are arranging a time, place, and space for learning, that is considered a "passive" program. Angela Hanscom, the author of *Balanced and Barefoot* and also the founder of Timbernook, has observed that it typically takes most children an average of forty-five minutes before they dive into deep play; they take that long to figure out who they are going to play with, decide what to do, and come up with a play strategy.[8] Thirty minutes of free play at the end of a program might not be enough. As the psychologist Peter Gray has observed:

> I've often seen such games ruined by well-meaning adults who intervened— for the sake of safety, or because they believed that someone was being treated unfairly, or because they believed that they knew better than the children how to make the game fun for children. Attentive adults can ruin games even if they don't intend to intervene. Children perceive them as potential enforcers of safety, solvers of conflicts, and audiences for whining; and this perception invites the children to act unsafely, to squabble, and to whine. Play requires self-control, and the too-obvious presence of adults can lead children to relinquish their self-control.[9]

Here's where the process-oriented learning we discussed in the first few chapters comes into play. By creating a rich, interesting environment and providing the tools kids need to be active and (relatively) safe, their imaginations will fill in the blanks. They will relax into the play and have fun. You can always pick out the kids who aren't used to this sort of play because they will either stay off to the side and take a long time before they decide to join the fray, or else they will be the ones I think of as "mini-dictators" (this was definitely me as a child), trying to control and orchestrate the whole game/craft/activity by lording it over everyone, assigning roles, or asking relentlessly for rules or guidance. Gently remind these tightly wound little darlings that this is "free play" and everyone is allowed to do whatever they want. Or preferably, don't say anything; just nod and smile and they will eventually huff off and figure it out on their own. Watch them slowly unwind as they get into their project or the collaborative play. Watch their faces relax, eventually. This is good. This is physical literacy. They are using their bodies as instruments, not ornaments. Their bodies and spirits are integrated, whole, and cohesive: immersed in play.

It's just as rewarding when you get to watch it happen with adults. Our weekly adult coloring group has bloomed to about twenty members (mostly seniors, a mix of genders), and sometimes I stand at the surveillance camera monitor and watch them all laughing and talking or serenely concentrating on their work in front of them. All we do is put out coloring books and pages, a pencil sharpener, and some markers and pencil crayons. Not everyone will experience a profound transformation from the experience of letting go in a group, but for some of our patrons it can be life-changing. One man who comes to our adult coloring program told me that before he joined our group he had been so depressed he rarely left the house, but now his favorite thing to do each week was to come to the library to color. They all go out for coffee afterwards to keep the fun going. He said that belonging to our group had saved him. The look of hope and joy and gratitude on his face brought tears to my eyes and a swelling of pride in my chest. You never know when a small thing you do will make such a big difference in the life of another human being. All I did was buy some supplies and advertise the event. They brought the heart.

You may have heard of the "loose parts" approach to play, a concept started by the architect Simon Nicholson—things that can easily be moved around the environment inspire creativity. Examples of such items could be wooden blocks and planks, sticks, rocks and pebbles, acorns, Lincoln Logs, Lego, cushions, blankets, pillows, dominos, cards, rope, yarn and string, shells, pinecones, Tinker Toys, beanbags, balls, baskets, clothespins, boxes, wooden dowels, and so on. Consider stationing some bins filled with these items in your children's department to encourage dramatic and sensory play. Putting out puzzles and board games is also good. Make sure you are welcoming to as many cultures as possible. Our puzzles have an Indigenous theme (figure 3.4), and one of our play carpets does too. Our board games come from all over the world. We have an after-school board game club where people can come and check out a game with their library card from our board game cart. We also offer the same thing as a monthly evening program for families to

FIGURE 3.4 First Nation puzzle

whom we provide a free healthy snack. We do a similar after-school program with Maker Boxes. We collect random recyclables, garbage and discards (think paper towel tubes, empty containers, clothespins, pipe cleaners, bits of cloth, wool and string, etc.), and throw them in bins. Once a week we put those bins out after school for students, and we encourage them to build something based on a theme like "magical monsters" or "tallest structure." By putting out paper, pencils, and old magazines next to your dress-up center (figure

FIGURE 3.5
Dress-up center

3.5), you can encourage children to improve their written literacy skills by making grocery lists, menus, and doctor's prescriptions, as well as taking appointments, creating their own currency, or any other imaginative ways children will put those props to good use.

Alternative Collections

I could write an entire book on alternative collections as they relate to physical literacy (maybe someday I will) because there are endless ideas. As most of you know, an alternative collection is a cataloged and labeled assortment of items that are not books (though it may contain books) that circulates either inside or outside the library. Possibly both. Most libraries now have DVDs, CDs, and other such items circulating regularly, something that was revolutionary only a few decades ago. Now alternative collections have gotten more diverse, from cake pans to power tools. Replacement costs and late fees apply, just like with print collections. In the program models in this book I give suggestions for alternative collections that match the program, but for now I'll just give a general list of what other libraries have created. Be sure to check out the sidebar for an example of a gym pass collection.

⟩ Sporting equipment and books/videos to accompany them. Right now I'm working on a partnership with our local nature reserve to buy snowshoes and include maps of the preserve for patrons to hike this winter. Some libraries create "fit kits" that combine multiple items with laminated cards of game ideas. These are great for individuals, families, day care centers, churches, and other community groups to borrow. Examples of other alternative formats you can lend: snowshoes, skis, ice cleats, yoga mats, kettle bells, Frisbees, parachutes, balls, skipping ropes, giant dice, plastic bowling sets, badminton or ping-pong sets, lawn games, fishing equipment, bicycle repair kits, binoculars, and camping gear. The possibilities are truly endless.

⟩ Board games, chess sets, and puzzles.

⟩ Fine motor activity kits, such as knitting, crocheting, robotics, electronics, and musical instruments.

⟩ Free passes to physical and cultural activities, such as museums, parks, play centers, gyms, swimming pools, canoe or bike rental shops, and dance, yoga, or Pilates studios.

Displays and Collections

The ultimate in passive advertising is creating fitness and movement-related book displays and adding the topics to your collections. Some of your patrons might not be lining up for a Zumba class, but subtly incorporating health and wellness displays in prominent locations in your library branch may give them the push they need to get moving. On my websites, I review many book titles and tell you whether they are worth adding to your collection, and there is a

Gwen Geiger Wolfe

Name: Gwen Geiger Wolfe, Information Services/
Health Librarian

Contact: ggeigerwolfe@lplks.org

Location: Lawrence Public Library, Lawrence, Kansas

Claim to Fame: The Health Spot, a partnership between a local hospital, the library, and other health-based organizations, as well as a physical spot to locate reliable health information, services, and more.

All-Star Program: GYM Pass Collection

In late 2015 I was having a conversation with a colleague and thought, "Wouldn't it be great if we could check out gym memberships?" And she said, "Yes! Why haven't we thought of that before?" And so the GYM Pass collection was born. I knew that I wanted to promote the opportunity for patrons to explore the use of gyms in the context of real life and make them more accessible. Many gyms offer a pass for two to seven days, but most people need more time to see how a gym could fit into their schedule—assuming they even like the gym and its resources—as well as to determine the logistics involved in making the commitment count. Not to mention opening up options for those individuals who would like to go to a gym but might not be able to afford it.

I started the project, as I do with most of my programming, with collaboration. I reached out to all of the local gyms in my community to see if they would be interested in partnering with my library to create the collection. I had three gyms respond; these were all local, single-location gyms that were eager to share this vision of openly accessible gyms to promote health and physical literacy. I met individually with each gym to determine their needs, gather their questions, and discuss the possibilities for the collection. I created a FAQ of their questions to share with each gym as we honed the nuts and bolts of managing gym memberships for checkout. Internally, I worked with multiple staff to establish a collection management policy, packaging, circulation rules, and responsibilities that were acceptable for all of the involved gyms and for the library.

continued on the following page ❱ ❱ ❱

continued from the previous page ❭❭❭

One of the biggest hurdles to a project like this is cost. Our library has been the recipient of a local health grant to support our health literacy programming and activities, which allowed us to successfully negotiate and pay for the gym memberships. Each pass for checkout represents one yearlong membership, to be shared among our patrons, and in our first year we had a total of four passes. The second year, however, we did not receive a grant, and so we needed to renegotiate our memberships in order to continue the collection. We were able to successfully spend half of what we paid the previous year and increase the collection by two memberships through donations and price reductions from each gym. We also established the expectation that this collection would grow over time and that each gym's participation was vital to the program's success.

Today, we have a continuous waiting list for our passes, as well as return patrons who are excited at the prospect of fitting healthy physical activity into their lives. Our next evolution will include moving the passes from a manual checkout procedure to adding it to our ILS and automated checkout system. The program has also made a model case for exploring more "Library of Things" collections, as well as inspiring our community to expect the unexpected from our library. The best moments are when patrons find out about our collection and we're able to visibly see their surprise and excitement as a new door opens to support their health goals.

list of recommended titles in this book's bibliography. Each program model in this book has a list of display selections in the section called "Multiple Literacy Tie-In." Get creative—the selections could be varied within each topic. For example, a "Running" display could include how-to running books, movies about runners, runner biographies, cookbooks for runners, and more.

Now that you've learned about some ways to sneak physical literacy initiatives into your existing spaces, let's move into creating some active indoor and outdoor programs. The next few chapters are separated by age demographics, but many of these programs can be modified for various age groups. Each program model is set up to include a description of the event, what you need to do in advance, what you need to do the day of the program, the budgetary requirements, the materials needed, some tips, variations on the theme, and, as mentioned above, some tie-ins with other forms of literacy, such as corresponding book displays or spinoff ideas.

Notes

1. Alex Soojung-Kim Pang, *Rest: Why You Get More Done When You Work Less* (New York: Basic Books, 2016).

2. Check it out at https://www.youtube.com/watch?v=E_HBGZVglv0.

3. This is the one I use: https://www.gaiam.com/products/classic-balance-ball-chair.

4. International Play Association, "Declaration on the Importance of Play," IPA World, 2014, http://ipaworld.org/wp-content/uploads/2015/05/IPA_Declaration-FINAL.pdf.

5. Anji Play World, "True Play: A Movement of Children, Teachers, Families, and Communities," Anji Play, 2017, www.anjiplay.com/home/#trueplay.

6. For an example, see http://kodokids.com/weaving-wall.

7. I review these decks at www.yogainthelibrary.com/yoga-for-children—teens.html.

8. To learn about Timbernook, visit www.timbernook.com/2017/index.html.

9. Peter Gray, "How to Ruin Children's Play: Supervise, Praise, Intervene," *Psychology Today*, 2009, https://www.psychologytoday.com/blog/freedom-learn/200901/how-ruin-children-s-play-supervise-praise-intervene.

Get the Sillies Out

Physical Literacy Programs for Children and Families

Have you ever noticed how eager young children are to learn about everything? And how they are constantly moving while doing so? Whether they are painting at an easel, stirring cake batter, or building blocks, their whole body is involved. And learning occurs during this movement.

—*Maureen Murdock*

When I started planning and delivering movement-based programs in libraries a decade ago, I didn't think too deeply about my motivation behind it. I started with yoga because yoga was what I knew, as a teacher and in my personal life. I had never been very good at sports and I often felt disconnected from my body, as if it was something that carried me around the world while my brain and heart did all the heavy lifting. When my first son was born, I suffered from postpartum obsessive-compulsive disorder; I seemed to be getting trapped more and more in my head, and the only thing that seemed to get me back into my body was practicing yoga and meditation as much as possible. I left the library service for a little while and started working with kids on the autism spectrum and with kids who had (sometimes severe) behavioral challenges, and one thing that consistently seemed to work was keeping these kids physically engaged. I would take them for walks to pick up trash on the playground, throw a ball around the yard, do some calming cross-lateral movements, or stretch to chill out. No matter what we did, movement seemed to be the key to regulating their often-fluctuating emotions and their subsequent out-of-control behavior. While some of their teachers and administrators saw these emotions and behaviors as "bad," and in need of punishment, or at least containment, I saw them as trying to *communicate a need.* The trick was to figure out what the need was and try to get that need met *before* the meltdown started. My curiosity about this led me down the rabbit hole of neurobiology and kinesiology, and I eventually came to the conclusion that we needed to address the *whole* child, and improving the child's physical literacy was a great place to start because children are naturally body-centric.

Fast-forward ten years and I've become a tireless promoter of physical literacy in my community, the library community at large, and to my own family and friends, because I know it works. I'm playing catch one Friday evening with my friend on the old middle school field in my neighborhood. We're talking about how good it feels to toss the ball around, how we could do it for hours, how we can feel our muscles remembering how to do something we hadn't done much of since we were kids. We discuss how neither of us had been particularly good at gym class as children or teens (we conclude it was due to our thick glasses prohibiting our involvement, not, of course, our inherent nerdiness). But we are both now fairly adept at a variety of sports (and wearing contacts), skills we had only recently acquired in our twenties and thirties. Then we point at each other and say, "Physical literacy!"

As the ball volleyed back and forth, we played around with making micro adjustments to our throws to see how accurate we could remain while tampering with certain variables, like tiny wrist flicks and stepping harder or softer on our front leg. We discussed how glad we felt that, despite being late developers, we had kept trying at sports. To anyone watching us, we just looked like two still-nerdy grownups playing catch.

And there *was* someone watching us. He was a kid about ten or eleven years old, a little overweight, who was hanging around his front yard across the street from the field. We saw him go inside and get his glove and start throwing the ball to himself. Some girls he knew walked by and he asked them to play, but they said no and wandered off. Then he came across the street and watched us in the park for about ten minutes, glove in hand, peeking out from behind the chain-link fence and bending over to pet a stray cat, nonchalantly.

I remembered being that kid. Out of shape, wanting desperately to be included, not having many other kids to play with, not being so good at sports either. So we invited him to play outfield while my friend pitched and I batted. We made sure he asked his parents first. I cheered when he made a decent throw, I hit as many balls in his direction as I could, and we gave him extra throws to give him more practice. We played until it got dark. We had a great time. We all improved our skills, young and not-so-young; and we built community, one neighbor at a time.

When adults and children play together, the level and variety of play that the child engages in rise.[1] By making the play collaborative and not controlled totally by the adults, the child also develops increased confidence and autonomy. Angela Hanscom insists that "as children play with each other, they learn how to negotiate, take turns, communicate effectively, listen, assert their needs, deal with conflicts, create and follow rules, and practice leadership skills."[2] Set a good example by being a mover. Change positions often during a program to prevent boredom, fidgeting, acting out, and pressures on the participants' joints from constant gravitational loads. Younger children will do this naturally, but by the time they reach middle school many have been conditioned to sit still at desks most of the day. You can counteract this. For example, during a craft program, have the kids stand up to introduce themselves and do an icebreaker; have the kids sit while you explain the craft and materials; walk in a circle around the table while generating ideas for what their project will look like; have the kids stand to work on some of the project, and sit for another part; take a stretch/yoga/dance break halfway through; and have the kids lie on their bellies in a circle to show each other their finished work and tell the story of their creation. You'll feel better too.

For the last few summers my library has hosted a Kids' Kilometer Fun Run (you can find the program model below). We have a great turnout. We partner with local businesses, police, and community organizations, and the families love it. It is free, accessible to anyone, and everyone gets to take home free books, fitness-related prizes, and fill their bellies with healthy food. Plus, we all get to take care of our bodies by doing some yoga and running/walking/rolling in the sunshine. If you are a public librarian, like me, you are probably not in it for the fame and fortune. But *this,* this memory-making and community-building, is my definition of success, and I bet it is yours too, or you wouldn't be reading this book. Cheering for every kid that crosses the finish line, able-bodied or not, cheering for that kid in the ball field when he makes a great throw, cheering for your struggling reader who is stringing a sentence together, that's what it is all about. Keep making it happen. Here are some ideas to get you started.

PROGRAM MODEL
Kids' Kilometer Fun Run

This is a big, annual event that involves your municipality, essential services, community groups, and businesses, and it usually draws a lot of positive attention from the press. It is a great way to get entire families involved in library programs; and if you give out picture and chapter books (or graphic novels) as prizes, it ties in textual/visual literacy as well. For those who would like to start with something smaller, see the "Variations" section below for more ideas.

FIGURE 4.1
Kids' Fun Run poster

Advance Planning

STEP 1. Talk to your library board and municipal officials to get the green light because this event will involve some fund-raising, planning with public works and essential services, and hopefully some promotional help from the tourism department (if you have one). Sports-related tourism is a big thing; it grosses $6.5 billion annually in Canada and $10.5 billion in the United States.[3]

STEP 2. Once you've got the go-ahead, pick a date and time. Saturdays and Sundays are the usual days for races. Morning, anywhere from 8 a.m. to 11 a.m. (depending on your geography), is best if you are running in the summer heat. You probably want to pick a time when your library is open, unless you are doing the run as an outreach project at a local park.

STEP 3. Plan your route. Our one-kilometer route leaves from the library parking lot and loops around a neighboring subdivision and comes back to the library. Work with the municipality and local police force to plan how to block off the streets to traffic. If this isn't possible due to your location, consider the possibility of holding the run at a local trail or park.

STEP 4. Contact your local health authority to alert them to the fact that a sporting event is taking place. Request that they send along some first responders to be on-site in case anyone is injured. In my town there is no cost to having medics on-site; check with your local health services. A volunteer nurse or doctor or anyone else trained in first aid is helpful.

STEP 5. Contact your local running club and get them involved. They more than likely already have lots of experience in planning races, if not as a club, then as individual volunteers at bigger events. This will also give you a ready-made set of participants. Not only do running club members love fun runs, they love anything that will get their friends and family running. They will be your best word-of-mouth promoters.

STEP 6. Decide if you want to require pre-registration, and if so, when the cut-off date for registering is. We ask people to pre-register so we can have an idea of how much food to buy and how many prizes to have, but we also accept people on the day of the event. We have a registration table where everyone needs to go to check in (if they've pre-registered) or sign up (if they haven't). Be prepared for a line to form.

STEP 7. Every parent/guardian and participant over age eighteen (check your local laws) who comes to your registration table needs to sign a liability waiver in case they get hurt during the race, so they can't sue the library or municipality and any of your partner organizations. Make these waivers ahead of time. Everyone also needs to sign a photo release waiver (or refusal) for photos and videos.

FIGURE 4.2 Book prizes

FIGURE 4.3 Run crowd

STEP 8. Invite the press. You're going to want to have coverage of such a big event, and the press loves a feel-good story about kids running a race and getting free books. Those smiles at the finish line (hopefully with your library in the background) look great on the front page of the paper.

STEP 9. Make sure you assign your own photographer to cover the event: a talented volunteer or staff member. You will want those pictures to help advertise the event next year. Plus you can share them on Facebook (pending approved photo releases) and get lots of likes and shares from the families that participated. They won't be able to take photos while they are running, and they'll appreciate having the memory recorded and available.

STEP 10. Decide what you are going to use for prizes. This isn't a real "race" in the sense that there are first, second, and third places. You could do that if you wanted to. We prefer to think of it as everyone gets a "finisher's medal." You can have real medals made up, but they are expensive, and they later collect dust or go to the landfill. What we do is ask a local business (a day care center) to donate books, or money to buy books, and we put a sticker in those books saying they are provided by that organization so the business gets a little advertising as a thank-you. Make sure the books are geared towards your target audience. If you have mostly young children signed up, you'll want lots of picture books and easy readers. If you have elementary school children,

FIGURE 4.4 Warm-up games

you'll want chapter books or graphic novels. I always throw a few young adult books onto the prize table because a number of teens join with their families. Other options for prizes include T-shirts, Frisbees, water bottles, bookmarks, ball caps, gift certificates to healthy restaurants, admission to local attractions, and so on. Work with local businesses to see if they will donate or sponsor your prizes. We are lucky to have a

FIGURE 4.5 Watermelon man

local financial business donate (branded) water bottles and Frisbees (that we also get the local running group logo on—next year we'll put the library logo on them!). We've also given out sunglasses. But this is always in addition to our books. The free books are the big attraction, and we focus on that.

STEP 11. I know these are a lot of steps. Big breath. If you get all the advance planning squared away, it will make race day so much easier. I promise. Unless it rains. That is step 11. Have a contingency plan. What are you going to do if the weather doesn't cooperate? Do you have an alternate date? Or can you postpone to later in the day? Is there a local indoor running track you could book as a backup? We've always been blessed with perfect northeast coast July weather, and our attitude is "rain or shine," but we would cancel the event in case of thunderstorms or high winds.

STEP 12. Plan what you are going to have for refreshments. At a bare minimum you have to offer water, enough water for everyone, even though many will bring their own. We also offer healthy fruit, like halved bananas, oranges (sliced or wedged), and watermelon. Sometimes we have fruit gummies for kids who don't like real fruit, but we try to stay away from those. You could have granola bars (nut-free is best), but then you have to deal with the wrappers on the ground. Contact your local grocers to see if they'd be willing to donate the food in exchange for their logo on the poster or a sign on the table. Our two local grocery stores always give us gift cards to buy whatever we want, and we send them a nice big thank-you letter. It is important to refuel with healthy food and water after physical activity, and having free food at this event works toward greater food security in your community. Leftovers can be donated to a local shelter or food bank that takes perishables. If you live in an urban area with a high homeless population using your facility, it's a good idea to leave the leftovers out on a table in your lobby (if you allow food in the building) or parking lot with a sign that says, "FREE! Take as much as you need." It will be gone in no time.

STEP 13. Recruit volunteers to help run the event. You're going to need people at the registration table, people along the route (preferably in neon safety vests), someone to sound the air horn/starting gun, people to look after the food and prizes, and someone to lead the warm-up and make announcements. You could also have someone at a table to register people for library cards or sign kids up for your summer reading program. One year we had a local bike club come and set up a table about their events, for some sporty cross-pollination. We've also had the local wellness organization involved. You could contact your local Rotary or other groups to see if they can help out. Your board members, regular library volunteers, staff, members of the local running club, and even high-school track students make great helpers. For our event, which has about 70 participants, we have about 10–15 people running the show (including police and ambulance services). The event itself doesn't last more than an hour, so this is a reasonable amount of time to ask someone to volunteer, and many people are happy to help.

STEP 14. Advertise. Don't forget to include the logos of your sponsors on your posters. Make a Facebook event. Tweet about the run. Do a call-in to the local radio station. Make sure to share advance word about the run with your local schools, day care centers, gyms, and sports clubs. Get your town's tourism department involved. Talk it up with the participating organizations to make sure their members know about it. Besides having uniformed police blocking off the street for us, we also have many police officers and their families who join in the event because word spreads among their members. They like to come cheer each other on.

Variations

▶ *Zombie Fun Run.* Volunteers dress up like zombies and "chase" (slowly, zombie-style) runners to the finish line. This is great for a nighttime program or around Halloween. It is not for the squeamish, however.

▶ *Reindeer Run.* This is done in December, and everyone wears Santa hats or reindeer antlers or elf hats (figure 4.6). Treats for finishers include hot chocolate, cookies, and candy canes. You can collect donations that will go to your local shelter to help others have a healthy and happy holiday. We do this every year and it is a blast—even in a snowstorm. I have the pictures to prove it.

▶ *Beer Run.* This caters to the twentysomething to thirtysomething crowd. If you can get a liquor license, everyone does a run (3–5 kilometers is best) and then comes back to the library to taste-test offerings from local breweries. This event might be best after hours, depending on your users or policies.

▶ *Obstacle Course.* If you've got a large parking lot or field nearby, this makes for a fun and challenging family event. Don't forget to include obstacles that can be overcome by people with limited mobility (Google "wheelchair obstacle course" for ideas).

FIGURE 4.6 Running reindeer

❱ **Storytime Run.** If a Kids' Kilometer Fun Run seems like a giant undertaking, why not incorporate a short sprint with the kids into your regular storytime? You can do a running-themed craft (Medals! Trophies!), read running related-picture books, such as

FIGURE 4.7 Bike safety

Marathon Mouse by Amy Dixon, and tell the tale of the Tortoise and the Hare with a felt board or puppet show. Fun! Can I come?

❱ **Bike Clinic.** Have a bike race or fun ride, obstacle course, and even on-site repairs. The local police can come teach about bike safety (figure 4.7). This is a very popular program at our library.

Materials Required

❏ Prizes (see step 10 of "Advance Planning" for ideas)

❏ Garbage cans

❏ Healthy snacks (see step 12 of "Advance Planning" for ideas)

❏ Platters/bowls for snacks

❏ Sharp knife for cutting fruit

❏ Tables (for registration, prizes, food, and any other booths you may want)

❏ Neon safety vests for volunteers to wear

❏ Sidewalk chalk to mark the route and the finish/starting line

❏ Air horn for starting gun (make sure it still has air)

❏ Liability waivers and photo releases

❏ Napkins or baby wipes (great for sticky fruit fingers)

❏ Water (either in bottles or in a big cooler with cups)

❏ First aid kit (if you don't have medics on-site)

❏ Megaphone (you may want to rent one if you aren't a loud talker like me)

Budget Details

$0-200+

I know you are looking at the $0 in the subhead above and are thinking, "Whaat? How?" This is where having good relationships with community partners and local businesses comes in. Plant the seeds, reap the benefits. At our event all the prizes are donated, all the food is donated, and the local running club supplies the volunteer vests and air horn. We do pay for things like garbage bags, napkins/baby wipes, and the paper we print the posters and waivers on, but they just come out of my regular operating budget, so I don't consider these a "special program" expense. I steal my kids' sidewalk chalk from home to mark the route.

If you are buying everything from scratch, it's going to add up. Based on a crowd of 50 people, refreshments (including napkins/baby wipes) are going to run you about $100, prizes (depending on what you give out) $100+, safety vest and megaphone rental $50, air horn $20, and chalk $3, putting you in the $250–300 range. Also keep in mind that you may be able to access grants for wellness programs or sports tourism. Check them out well in advance to make sure you apply before the deadline and secure funding.

Day of the Event

STEP 1. Gather volunteers and assign tasks so everyone knows what they are doing.

STEP 2. Set up tables, cut up fruit, and put out refreshments and prizes. Set up the registration booth and any other booths you plan on having.

STEP 3. Call police and first responder contacts to confirm what time they will arrive.

STEP 4. Use sidewalk chalk to mark the course. Set up the finish line. Have volunteers ready along the route in their safety vests.

STEP 5. As people begin arriving have them register, sign waivers, and gather near the starting line.

STEP 6. Before the starting gun, lead everyone in a big stretch session to limber up. Explain the route and procedures. Point out the first aid station and what to do in case of emergency or injury.

STEP 7. Have fun. Enjoy watching families milling around afterwards chatting in the (fingers crossed!) sunshine and the kids looking at their new books.

STEP 8. Clean up. Regroup with volunteers and debrief. Make a list of what went well and do-betters for next year.

Tips

1. If you're going to order T-shirts, consider that you'll need a wide variety of sizes. I highly recommend a pre-registration-only setup if you are going to order T-shirts.

2. Stand at the finish line to cheer on the stragglers. It is hard to come in last. You don't have to embarrass them with over-the-top antics, but make sure they have a little fanfare.

3. Make sure your air horn has enough pressure. I cannot stress this enough. Nothing is more disappointing than blowing the starting gun with a crowd of people eagerly watching you and nothing but a *hiss* comes out.

4. Keep an eye on the weather. Have a backup plan and a way to let everyone know what the plan is. You don't want people showing up at the wrong place, or coming to the event if it is canceled.

5. Make sure people have access to washrooms. Drinking lots of water and being excited/nervous makes everyone need to pee more, especially if they've been eating watermelon.

6. If you're in a very multicultural community, it is helpful to have volunteers who speak multiple languages on-site to help translate directions and instructions for participants. Or you can make signs and banners in multiple languages. For example, if you have a large Spanish-speaking audience, it is helpful and respectful to make the announcements in both English and Spanish, if possible. And since it is a family event, if older generations have come along, they may not speak English as well as their children. For the waivers, keep in mind that it may not be legally binding to have someone sign a waiver in a language they don't fully understand, so you may want to have them translated. Know your audience and prepare accordingly.

7. Make sure the route is wheelchair, stroller, and other mobility device-friendly so that as many people are possible can participate. Try it out yourself by taking a wagon, stroller, or a shopping cart for a spin in advance; you may find issues with curbs or potholes you wouldn't have noticed if you were relying solely on your legs.

8. It's hard to hand out evaluation forms after this program, with everyone leaving at different times and being outdoors and having a lack of writing surfaces. If they are asked to give their e-mail on the registration form, you could add a check box asking "Do you mind if we contact you for follow-up after this program? Yes/No," and then e-mail them the evaluation form or create an online anonymous survey through software like SurveyMonkey.

Multiple Literacy Tie-In

❭ You can create some awesome collection displays for participants to browse before or after the program (make sure to use multiple formats—audio, text, braille, DVDs, etc.)

Books about movement-based play, such as:
- *Learning with the Body in Mind: The Scientific Basis for Energizers, Movement, Play, Games, and Physical Education,* by Eric Jensen
- *Making the Brain-Body Connection,* by Sharon Promislow
- *Move, Play, and Learn with Smart Steps: Sequenced Activities to Build the Body and the Brain,* by Gill Connell, Wendy Pirie, and Cheryl McCarthy
- *A Moving Child Is a Learning Child: How the Body Teaches the Brain to Think,* by Gill Connell and Cheryl McCarthy
- *Smart Moves: Why Learning Is Not All in Your Head,* by Carla Hannaford

❭ You can display books, periodicals, and films about sports, especially running or biographies of runners. Depending on the size of your library, you could have one book display in your teen department, one in the children's department, and another display for adults.

For youth
- *The Girl Who Ran: Bobbi Gibb, The First Women to Run the Boston Marathon,* by Frances Poletti and Kristina Yee
- *Good Sports: Rhymes about Running, Jumping, Throwing, and More,* by Jack Prelutsky
- *Izzy Barr, Running Star,* by Claudia Mills
- *Jesse Owens,* by Laurie Calkhoven
- *Kid Athletes: True Tales of Childhood from Sports Legends,* by David Stabler
- *Marathon Mouse,* by Amy Dixon
- *Run with Me: The Story of a U.S. Olympic Champion,* by Sanya Richards-Ross
- *Running the Road to ABC,* by Denize Lauture
- *Strong Is the New Pretty: A Celebration of Girls Being Themselves,* by Kate T. Parker

- *Wilma Unlimited: How Wilma Rudolph Became the World's Fastest Woman*, by Kathleen Krull

For adults

- *Born to Run: A Hidden Tribe, Superathletes, and the Greatest Race the World Has Never Seen*, by Christopher McDougall
- *Build Your Running Body: A Total-Body Fitness Plan for All Distance Runners, from Milers to Ultramarathoners—Run Farther, Faster, and Injury-Free*, by Pete Magill et al.
- *Eat and Run: My Unlikely Journey to Ultramarathon Greatness*, by Scott Jurek
- *Running with the Mind of Meditation: Lessons for Training Body and Mind*, by Sakyong Mipham
- *The Running Revolution: How to Run Faster, Farther, and Injury-Free—for Life*, by Nicholas Romanov and Kurt Brungardt

Periodicals

- *Canadian Running Magazine*
- *Men's Running Magazine*
- *Runner's World*
- *Trail Runner*
- *Women's Running Magazine*

Films

- *The Athlete* (2009)
- *Desert Runners* (2013)
- *Forrest Gump* (1994)
- *Free to Run* (2016)
- *From Fat to Finish Line* (2015)
- *Into the Wind* (2010)
- *Prefontaine* (1997)
- *Run Fatboy Run* (2007)
- *Run Lola Run* (1998)
- *Saint Ralph* (2004)
- *Ultramarathon Man: 50 Marathons, 50 States, 50 Days* (2008)
- *Without Limits* (1998)

❭ A display of any fitness-related alternative collections: pedometers, yoga mats, gym passes, fit kits, workout DVDs, kettlebells, Frisbees, and so on.

PROGRAM MODEL
Healthy Nutrition for Families

Taking care of your body (inside and out) and being able to read its hunger, satiation, and nutritional cues is part of well-developed physical literacy. This fun and flexible program can help your patrons develop these skills. Parents/guardians learn about healthy nutrition from a guest speaker while their kids get some exercise while sampling healthy treats.

Advance Planning

FIGURE 4.8
Healthy Nutrition poster

STEP 1. Figure out what time of day and what day of the week you want to run the program. Do you want to coordinate it with National Nutrition Month (March)? The timing may be dependent on when your guest speaker is available. Evenings and weekends are good for families where parents work 9–5 jobs, but homeschool families or shift-work and work-at-home families might be available during the day—you know your crowd best. Maybe you could offer it twice? Once you've got a date nailed down, book the room. The program will last one hour. You're going to want to use either two rooms close together or a room with a dividing wall. Do you want this to be a drop-in program or do you want pre-registration?

STEP 2. Track down a nutritionist, dietician, or holistic health consultant who would be happy to volunteer an hour of their time to give a presentation at your library. There are often government-funded agencies that are only too happy to send someone out. Another alternative is getting someone from your local health food store to come give a talk, or perhaps even someone on the board of a local farmers market. You can decide what direction you'd like to take the program based on your community—you're probably going to get wildly different food perspectives in, say, Boulder, Colorado than you will in Houston, Texas or Alert, Nunavut. Also, depending on how you spin the talk, you may get a totally different crowd. Just make sure you are getting a speaker with a well-rounded, firm, scientific grasp of healthy nutrition and who isn't hawking their vitamin supplements or telling everyone that eating meat is the basis of our impending global collapse (that can be a totally different talk—see "Variations" below). The event is not meant to be political, or spark debate; it is meant to inform and explore.

STEP 3. You're going to need to get some groceries, so make a list (see the "Materials Required" section for ideas). This is the fun part. While the guest speaker is giving their talk to the adults, you (or the lovely staff members you have recruited for this) are going to take the kids into another room for an awesome game. The game is really simple and kids *love* it. Get the food ahead of time and make sure you have time to prep it (i.e., cut it up, put it on platters/bowls, and so on).

STEP 4. Another thing you have to make sure of ahead of time is that the parents have signed a waiver telling you if their child has any allergies, has permission to eat food and exercise, and is old enough not to choke on small pieces of food (usually ages three and up, but you decide what you feel comfortable with; I would probably say ages five and up so I don't have to deal with toddlers). Make the waivers, they are important.

STEP 5. You'll need a big piece of Bristol board and some markers because you're going to make a chart (this is a great job to give to a summer student or arty volunteer). On this chart you're going to draw or paste a picture of a fruit or vegetable (this will depend on your grocery shopping). Each food item is going to have a corresponding action, which you'll make up with the kids on the day of the event. It is also a good idea to have some water bottles or a fountain handy in case they get thirsty.

STEP 6. Find out if your state/province/governing body has a food handling policy and adhere to it. My staff and volunteers have been certified in a nationally recognized food handler program and are well-versed in food safety.

Variations

❱ *Local Food Hunt.* Visit a farm, community garden, or perhaps your library's own garden and taste-test the things growing there. If you have a local herbalist or mushroom hunter, you could even go exploring to taste things in the wild. I did this at a local day care center by bringing a variety of potted herbs to smell and taste. Afterwards the kids planted them.

❱ *Food Scrambler.* If you don't want to or can't (because of policies) have food in your library, have the kids cut out pictures of different kinds of food from old magazines and sort them into piles of what is healthy and what is

not. Buy three Bristol boards and
label them "Healthy," "Not
Healthy," and "Once in a While,"
and have the kids glue the pictures
on to the boards. When you get to
something questionable, like pizza,
for example, use that as an opportunity to discuss what sorts of
toppings can make pizza healthier
or not so healthy. When you get to
something like soda, discuss
whether it should go in the "Not

FIGURE 4.9 Healthy nutrition

Healthy" or "Once in a While" category and why. If the group can't decide,
put one on both boards. Try not to get into polarizing discussions; just use
this exercise as an opportunity to let the kids explore and question previously held beliefs. Cutting and glueing are excellent opportunities to practice fine motor skills in younger children. Show off their hard work to the
parents once they are done listening to your guest speaker (if you have one).

❩ ***Teen Tasting.*** Run a similar program for a young adult audience. Have the
nutritionist give a short talk, cut out food items from magazines, have a
discussion about their nutritional value, and then try eating some different
fruits and vegetables, ranking which ones they liked the best and why.

Materials Required

❏ Bristol board and markers, with food items compiled in a clear chart for
reference during the activity. Or you can make a digital version and project it
on a screen, if you have the technology available.

❏ A garbage can/compost bucket for rejected offerings and peels/rinds, napkins, and so on.

❏ Water bottles or cups for tap water or access to a fountain.

❏ Napkins/paper towels.

❏ Liability waivers and photo release forms.

❏ Evaluation forms.

❏ Platters/plates/bowls for the food, and knives to cut it up, and a cutting board.

❏ Food. You can either play it safe or get really creative here. How much variety
do you want to offer? How many people do you expect will attend? What's

in-season and abundant in your area? What's exotic and fun to try that kids' parents might not offer at home (due to price or reluctance)? Here are some ideas:

Vegetables (or fruits that people consider vegetables)

- Cherry tomatoes
- Broccoli (florets)
- Button mushrooms
- Mini-carrots (or sticks)
- Celery (sticks)
- Cauliflower (florets)
- Cabbage (sliced; red or green)
- Beets (shredded or julienned)
- Kale (torn into pieces)
- Radish (sliced)
- Cucumber (sliced)
- Green beans
- Sugar-snap peas
- Bell pepper (sliced)
- Parsley (torn into pieces)
- Parsnip (shredded or julienned)
- Onion (sliced, try Vidalia—it's sweet)
- Sprouts (alfalfa, radish, broccoli)
- Mung bean sprouts (these are bigger)
- Water chestnuts (sliced, canned)
- Avocado (sliced)
- Beet greens (torn into pieces or leaves)
- Baby spinach (leaves)
- Endive (individual leaves)
- Turnip (sticks)
- Fennel (sliced)
- Corn (canned, kernels)
- Mustard greens (individual leaves)

Fruit

- Kiwi (sliced)
- Watermelon (sliced or chunks)
- Mango (sliced or chunks; frozen or regular)
- Strawberries (husked)
- Blueberries
- Raspberries
- Blackberries
- Gooseberries
- Cherries
- Banana (sliced)
- Pineapple (chunks)
- Apple (sliced)
- Pear (sliced)
- Peach (sliced)
- Orange (sliced)
- Grapes
- Grapefruit (sliced)
- Papaya (sliced)
- Figs (quartered)
- Dates (pitted)
- Pomegranate seeds
- Coconut (chunks)
- Lychee (let them peel them—so fun!)
- Prunes
- Honeydew melon (sliced)
- Cantaloupe (sliced)
- Starfruit (sliced)
- Cranberries (dried or fresh)

Budget Details

$0–100

If you can secure funding through a wellness, nutrition, or food-security grant, you could possibly have zero expenses for this program. We hardly ever pay for food for our programs due to the generosity of our local farmers, grocers, and government wellness branch. You can ask families to bring their own tableware. Otherwise, it is going to cost you between $50 and $100 for the food, napkins, and plates, depending on the size of your crowd. I recommend buying as much food as you can from local farmers markets, so you know it is fresh and you are supporting your community members. As mentioned above, you should be able to track down a dietician, nutritionist, or health consultant to present to the adults for free; check with your local health authority, health stores, or government wellness programs.

Day of the Event

STEP 1. Cut up all your fruits and veggies and put them on platters or bowls. Set out the napkins and drinks. Put up your poster boards or projection.

STEP 2. Prepare your room for the guest speaker and whatever equipment they need (mic, projector, etc.). Make sure to test all the equipment ahead of time.

STEP 3. As families arrive, have them gather in the room the parents will be in. Introduce the guest speaker and explain the program. Have the parents/guardians sign the liability waiver and photo release. Invite the parents/guardians to feel free to join in either activity, so if they want to accompany their child they feel comfortable doing so.

STEP 4. Take the kids into their room. Explain the game to the kids and get them to come up with some actions to go with each food item you have to taste-test. Write them on the big chart you made. Here's some ideas to get you started: kiwi slice = frog hop; watermelon slice = run in place to the count of ten; carrot stick = push-up; banana slice = five sit-ups; celery stick = dance in place; apple slice = slither like a snake; pineapple chunk - five jumping jacks; button mushroom = touch head, belly, toes five times; mango slice = pretend to swim; raspberry = gallop like a horse. The kids will have great ideas for silly ways to move!

STEP 6. The kids will try a piece of food and then do the corresponding action. Make sure the rules are *very* clear that all food must be *chewed* and *swallowed* before the action can begin. This isn't a race, it's an exploration. The more exotic the fruits and vegetables, the better, so kids can try things out of their comfort zone. Have a garbage can handy so they can spit out things they don't like. Remember to have some water bottles or a fountain handy in case they get thirsty. The kids go at their own pace, and no one is forced to try anything they don't want to.

STEP 7. Let the kids keep playing the game until the food runs out. Have them take turns pointing to their favorite and least favorite items on the chart. There is no "winner" in the game; the goal is just to have fun trying new things and getting some exercise. Have the kids help clean up and then bring them back to their parents/guardians.

STEP 8. Have the kids tells their parents all the yummy things they tried and what their favorite or least favorite item was. Have them demonstrate the corresponding movement too. Now is a good time to hand out evaluation forms to the adults to fill out if you're using them.

Tips

1. If you have differently-abled kids in attendance, make sure there are corresponding exercises that everyone can achieve.

Multiple Literacy Tie-In

Here are some display and collection development ideas:

⟩ Family or kid-oriented cookbooks. Here are some of my favorites:

- *But My Family Would Never Eat Vegan! 125 Recipes to Win Everyone Over*, by Kristy Turner
- *The Cookbook for Kids: Great Recipes for Kids Who Love to Cook*, by Lisa Atwood
- *Cooking Class: 57 Fun Recipes Kids Will Love to Make (and Eat!)*, by Deanna F. Cook
- *Everyday Kitchen for Kids: 100 Amazing Savory and Sweet Recipes Children Can Really Make*, by Jennifer Low
- *Feeding the Whole Family: Cooking with Whole Foods: More Than 200 Recipes for Feeding Babies, Young Children, and Their Parents*, by Cynthia Lair
- *The Help Yourself Cookbook for Kids: 60 Easy Plant-Based Recipes Kids Can Make to Stay Healthy and Save the Earth*, by Ruby Roth
- *How to Feed a Family: The Sweet Potato Chronicles Cookbook*, by Laura Keogh and Ceri Marsh
- *Kid Chef: The Foodie Kids Cookbook: Healthy Recipes and Culinary Skills for the New Cook in the Kitchen*, by Melina Hammer
- *Little Bento: 32 Irresistible Bento Box Lunches for Kids*, by Michele Olivier
- *Plant-Powered Families: Over 100 Kid-Tested, Whole-Foods Vegan Recipes*, by Dreena Burton

○ *The School Year Survival Cookbook: Healthy Recipes and Sanity-Saving Strategies for Every Family and Every Meal (Even Snacks)*, by Laura Keogh and Ceri Marsh

❱ Some libraries have alternative collections of cookware or bakeware; this would be a great tie-in.

❱ Food-related DVDs such as:

○ *Cloudy with a Chance of Meatballs 1 & 2* (2009, 2013)
○ *Fat, Sick & Nearly Dead* (2010)
○ *Food Inc.* (2008)
○ *Forks over Knives* (2001)
○ *The Hundred-Foot Journey* (2014)

○ *Hungry for Change* (2012)
○ *Julie & Julia* (2009)
○ *Ratatouille* (2007)
○ *Super Size Me* (2004)
○ *What's On Your Plate?* (2009)

PROGRAM MODEL **Family Dance Party**

FIGURE 4.10
Family Dance Party poster

Are you looking for a great way to get families physically active at your library without offering structured sports programs? How about a fun way to combine physical literacy with verbal and music literacy? It's time for you to host a Family Dance Party.

Advance Planning

STEP 1. Pick a date and time for the event. During the day works for stay-home or shift-work families, day cares, and the after-school crowd. Evenings might work, but you have to remember that a lot of children are in scheduled weekly activities in the evenings, especially during the school year. Weekend mornings or afternoons are often good times for families. Decide if you are going to have pre-registration or if it will be a drop-in program. Decide how long the program will last: 30–60 minutes is good.

STEP 2. Advertise. Make a poster, put it on your event calendar and website, make a Facebook event, and don't forget word of mouth. An enthusiastic

Summer Reading Club Leader can promote the event to members during regularly scheduled SRC events. You could even make a little YouTube dance video.

STEP 3. Decide where you are going to hold the dance party and what items you will need. We have our dance parties in a multipurpose activity room. If you don't have such a space, you could hold it in the children's department or even outside using a portable stereo system. Purchase a bunch of balloons if you are doing it indoors. Bubbles are good too. You can rent a bubble machine or just get a bunch of bubbles and wands. You can also rent a dance light from a local music store that could be set to pulsate colors. This light can be propped up and projected onto a wall. How about a disco ball? Hula hoops? Gather a laptop and a set of computer speakers, or a portable stereo, or a Bluetooth speaker and MP3 player. Make sure this gear is working and is loud enough in the room or outside. You don't want to find out that your sound system doesn't work only a few minutes before the event.

STEP 4. Decide if you want refreshments and purchase them. How about some punch, water, Popsicles, or Freezies?

STEP 5. Create liability waivers and photo release forms if you plan on taking pictures or a video for use on your library's website or Facebook page (which is a good idea if your policies allow it; dancing kids are adorable and you'll get lots of "likes").

STEP 6. Choose your playlist. This can either be a video playlist created on YouTube or an audio playlist on your device. It's best to have music that appeals to a wide age group if you don't know who is coming. Music from movies or TV shows is very popular. Watch out for swear words or violent/sexual content. You can't please everyone, but play songs for some teachers or parents you know in order to see if they'd let their kids listen to them. Ask the staff for suggestions, and no doubt they will show off some of their best dance moves for you. There is a sample playlist found in the "Materials Required" section below.[4] No one has complained about our playlist, but that's no guarantee. Make sure the playlist is longer than the time of the dance, so any songs that aren't jiving with the crowd can be skipped (or in case everyone is having so much fun they don't want to leave!). You might want to check with your administration about whether or not you need permission to play copyrighted music during an event. In Canada we have permission to play legally acquired music publicly so long as we are a nonprofit entity and it is for educational purposes.[5] It would be the same as music being played during gym class at school.

FIGURE 4.11 Family Dance Party

Variations

❭ *Dance, Dance Revolution Party.* If you've already got the setup for it—go for it!

❭ *Lunch Break Dance Party.* If you run a school library, offer a dance party during lunch hour on a rainy day.

❭ *Stress-Break Dance Party.* During finals week in your academic library, bust out some moves with the students to help them de-stress. Short, 15–30-minute sessions are best, so the students won't get too distracted from their work.

❭ *Back-to-Class Dance Party.* Host a fun frolic during the first week back to school in order to let everyone meet some new people and loosen up.

❭ *Glow Dance Party.* Buy a bunch of glow sticks, get a black light, and have everyone wear white. Black out the windows, turn off the lights, and bust out the moves! This is an extremely popular event at our library, and I highly recommend it.

❭ *After-School Dance Party.* This is a great way for kids to unwind after a long day at their desks. We invited all ages and offered it as a six-week program at our library, and it was well-attended. We will definitely do it again.

❭ *Rompin' Stompin' Storytime.* See the sidebar for more information.

Lisa Hartzell

Name: Lisa Hartzell, Youth Services Librarian

Contact: lhartzell@haywoodnc.net

Location: Haywood County Public Library, North Carolina

Claim to Fame: Music and movement programs

All-Star Program: Rompin' Stompin' Storytime

My colleague sent me a box of discarded instruments (shakers, rhythm sticks, tambourines, etc.), and I thought it would be fun to somehow incorporate these into a storytime. I know we have all heard of Kindermusik programs, which can be costly, and I thought it would be great to do something similar. I started looking around on the Internet for some inspiration, and I surveyed parents to find a good day and time. We would still read books, but the main focus would be on music and movement. I liked the idea of merging literacy with movement. In the beginning it was a lot of trial and error, but I was able to find some great ideas.

I searched the Internet for activities and for music and found two really great websites.[6] I tried many songs and found some that the kids really loved. It was also easy to see what they didn't like, too. It's a very fast-paced program, so when you see them start to lose attention, you just switch to something else.

We purchased beanbags, ribbons, stretchy bands, and a parachute to go along with the instruments. I would have to say the most popular activity is the parachute. The kids love getting under it while the parents walk around moving it up and down to nursery rhymes or songs like "London Bridge" or "Ring Around the Rosie." Another favorite is adding balls or even pom-poms and letting them fly everywhere. This has become our most popular storytime with around 20–30 kids on average, which in our small community is wonderful. It continues to grow as parents spread the word. We offer a similar storytime, Movers and Shakers, at our main branch, and this is also one of our most popular programs, averaging twenty-five kids.

I love the fact that the children are improving their motor skills and coordination. I try to incorporate books that encourage interaction and participation. The best part is that kids are allowed to move and make a little noise. We ended up with a program that is a full hour of singing, dancing, and exercise and is loads of fun.

Materials Required

- ❏ Refreshments: water, Freezies, Popsicles, punch
- ❏ Cups for punch, if needed
- ❏ Napkins or baby wipes
- ❏ Garbage can
- ❏ Bubbles or bubble machine
- ❏ Strobe light, disco ball, or light machine (warn people ahead of time, because some people get seizures from bright, flashing lights)
- ❏ Balloons
- ❏ Hula hoops
- ❏ Portable stereo, Bluetooth speaker and device, or laptop and speakers
- ❏ Liability waivers
- ❏ Photo release forms and camera (if using)
- ❏ Music

  Sample Playlist:[7]
  - ◦ *Crazy Frog,* by Axel F
  - ◦ *U Can't Touch This,* by MC Hammer
  - ◦ *Gangnam Style,* by PSY
  - ◦ *Let It Go,* by Frozen
  - ◦ *In the Jungle,* by Madagascar
  - ◦ *I Like to Move It,* by Madagascar
  - ◦ *Happy,* by Pharrell Williams (Ft. Minions)
  - ◦ *Call Me Maybe,* by Carly Rae Jepsen
  - ◦ *What Does the Fox Say?* by Ylvis
  - ◦ *Everything Is Awesome!,* by The Lego Movie
  - ◦ *Cha Cha Slide,* by Mr. C The Slide Man
  - ◦ *Dancing Queen,* by ABBA
  - ◦ *Who Let the Dogs Out,* by Baha Men
  - ◦ *Peanut Butter Jelly Time,* by Chipman
  - ◦ *Celebrate,* by Kool and the Gang
  - ◦ *Shake It Off,* by Taylor Swift
  - ◦ *I'm a Believer,* by Smash Mouth (*Shrek* soundtrack)
  - ◦ *Stayin' Alive,* by the Bee Gees
  - ◦ *Uptown Funk,* by Mark Ronson Ft. Bruno Mars
- ❏ Parent evaluation forms (if using)

Budget Details

$0–200

This can be a fairly low-budget program, depending on the options you choose. If you just play music on an existing device with no additional props, it could even be free. The cost to rent a bubble machine is anywhere from $30 to $200, depending on whether you get a small, plastic one or a large industrial machine. A disco ball or strobe light rental is going to run you in the $10–50 range, depending on how fancy you get. Balloons shouldn't cost more than $5. Regular bubbles should be in the $5–10 range, depending on how many bottles you buy. Refreshments could be anywhere from free (tap water from a fountain) to $15 for a big box of Freezies. Hula hoops are at the dollar store, usually. Napkins or baby wipes should be in the $5 range. A stereo and camera rental or purchase is going to put you well over the $200 threshold, but I'm working from the assumption that most libraries have something already available, or could borrow one from a volunteer or staff member.

Day of the Event

STEP 1. Blow up the balloons (if using). Get the bubbles and hula hoops ready.

STEP 2. Put out refreshments, cups (if using), napkins/wipes, and garbage can. If you are going to give out Freezies, hold off until halfway through the Dance Party.

STEP 3. Check the sound system and lights to make sure everything is working fine and the volume is good.

STEP 4. Don't forget the waivers and photo releases (if using) and either set up a table at the door to make sure every family signs, or have a clipboard for when they arrive.

STEP 5. Put the music on and let the fun begin!

STEP 6. Hand out the evaluation forms for parents and guardians to complete, if using.

Tips

1. It is really essential to have some props. You can even raid your existing storytime tickle trunk for some shakers, felt squares, streamers, beanbags, and so on. Remember how we talked about the "loose parts" movement and free play? Just put stuff out and the kids will explore it. Everyone will be a little awkward at first, and giving the kids (and parents) something to play with will loosen them up. They'll go from bopping balloons to a conga line in no time!

2. If your audience isn't feeling the tunes, feel free to skip to the next song—you want to keep them groovin'!

Multiple Literacy Tie-In

Create some great displays of items that participants can check out after the program, and don't forget to include multiple formats (audio, text, braille, DVDs, etc.).

❭ CDs geared towards kids. Movie soundtracks are always a hit. Here's some good ones that are also (mostly) tolerable for parents:

- *A Family Album,* by The Verve Pipe
- *Frog Trouble,* by Sandra Boynton
- *Here Comes the 123's,* by They Might Be Giants
- *Muppets: The Green Album,* by various artists
- *Pioneer Lane,* by The Watson Twins
- *Recess,* by Justin Roberts
- *Rocket Ship Beach,* by Dan Zane
- *Sing-a-Longs & Lullabies for the Film Curious George,* by Jack Johnson and Friends
- *Snack Time!* by The Barenaked Ladies
- *Soulville: Soul Stuff for Kids of All Ages,* by Little Monsters Records
- *You Are My Little Bird,* by Elizabeth Mitchell

❭ Books and films about different kinds of dance (ballroom, tribal, belly dance, highland dance, ballet, hip-hop, tap dance, etc.). You could also have dance workout DVDs. For narrative films, here's some ideas to get you started:

- *Annie* (1982, 2014)
- *Billy Elliot* (2000)
- *Center Stage* (2000)
- *Happy Feet* (2006)
- *High School Musical* (2006)
- *Save the Last Dance* (2001)
- *Singin' in the Rain* (1952)
- *Step Up* (2006)
- *Swing Kids* (1993)

❱ Biographies of famous dancers or performers. You could have one display for adults and one for youth. Here are a few ideas:

For youth:

° *Josephine: The Dazzling Life of Josephine Baker,* by Patricia Hruby Powell

° *Rap a Tap Tap: Here's Bojangles—Think of That!* by Leo Dillon and Diane Dillon

° *Swan: The Life and Dance of Anna Pavlova,* by Laurel Snyder

For adults:

° *Katherine Dunham: Dance and the African Diaspora,* by Joanna Dee Das

° *Life in Motion: An Unlikely Ballerina,* by Misty Copeland

° *Mao's Last Dancer,* by Li Cunxin

❱ Films with music from your playlist, such as:

° *Frozen* (2013)

° *The Lego Movie* (2014)

° *Madagascar* (2005)

PROGRAM MODEL **A Wild Rumpus**

This is a re-creation of the rambunctious parade from Maurice Sendak's famous children's book Where the Wild Things Are. *It is a fun, silly event for all ages that encourages active free play while maintaining a thematic structure with a strong literary base.*[8]

FIGURE 4.12
Wild Rumpus poster

Advance Planning

STEP 1. Decide where and when you are going to have the event. Indoors it can be offered all year long, but it would also be a fun outdoor activity if you have the available space. Pick a time when families with young children will be most available; a weekend afternoon or evening works well.

STEP 2. Decide if it is going to be a drop-in program or require pre-registration (this makes it easier to know how many crowns to prepare and snacks to buy).

FIGURE 4.13 King

STEP 3. Plan your activities and gather and prepare supplies (see the "Materials Required" section). Here are some activity suggestions; feel free to do some or all of them (or make up your own):

❳ *Max Crowns:* Everyone is going to want a sweet paper crown like Max wears in the book. You can make a bunch of precut templates that the kids can decorate themselves with whatever you have on hand (markers, glitter glue, pom-poms, stickers, ribbons, stick-on jewels), and then just size them to their heads.[9] Or you can just put out a bunch of construction paper and notions and let them freestyle their own crowns. This is a good option if you didn't have a pre-registration and you have no idea how many people will show up. If you are an ardent literary enthusiast and desperately want everyone's crowns to look Max-like for consistency, choose the appropriate template.

❳ *Storytime:* This activity isn't really optional; you pretty much *have* to read *Where the Wild Things Are*. Heck, if you wanted to make this program a full-day event, you could even show the movie afterward and have popcorn. After all, if you are going to do something and you have the time and resources, you may as well go all-in.

❳ *Free Play Dance Mash-Up:* This is where things get super fun. Pick a location that has a giant open area. Fill this open area with the following:

FIGURE 4.14 Rumpus

large sheets of fabric, hula hoops, giant blocks, empty cardboard boxes, child-friendly musical instruments, and balls or balloons. Now here's the scary part for you lovers of structure and routine: you are going to do nothing. Prepare to play some music (see the "Materials Required" section for a pre-fab playlist) and let the kids have at it. They are going to make a mess. Well, it will look like a mess to you, but it will actually be a brilliant, creative, organic fantasyland of awesomeness. This is okay (hyperventilate into a bag in the corner if necessary). At first the becrowned kiddos may stand off to the side awkwardly, unsure that they are really allowed to do *whatever they want* with the bounty before them. But worry not, within three to five minutes you will have some little human standing on a box and smashing it, another little human rocking out with a tambourine, and a ragtag band of misfits working together to build an awesome castle complete with fabric moat and hula hoop turrets. It will be loud, so you may wish to supply earplugs for the parents/staff (and apologize to the patrons on the other side of the closed door who may be trying to read or do their taxes).

❱ **Noisemakers:** If you don't already possess an ample supply of noisemakers (sand eggs, tambourines, triangles, jingle bells, maracas, rattles, shakers, etc.), part of the fun can be making some. Decorate some toilet paper tubes, cover one end with wax paper circles and an elastic band, drop in a handful of dried beans or split-peas, cover the other end with a circle of wax paper, and pop an elastic band on. Ta-da! Instant headache-inducing awesomeness.[10]

❭ **Wild Walk:** Take your kings and queens of the wild things on a magic parade through the library or outside. Bring along noisemakers, make your best growls and howls, and stomp your feet and gnash your teeth. Bonus points for finding as many weird and wild ways to walk (or roll) as possible.

❭ *Rumpus Refreshments:* Your wild things will get very hungry with all their active play, so be sure to have some snacks on hand like goldfish crackers, green grapes, and carrot sticks. Monsters especially like to stick Bugles on their fingers like claws.[11]

STEP 4. Based on the activities you've chosen, plan how much time you'll need. This program could be an hour, or it could easily be an entire afternoon.

STEP 5. Prepare liability waivers, photo/video releases, and evaluations (if using).

STEP 6. Advertise! Make a great poster and put it up in local day care centers, churches, schools, and other public gathering places for families. Make an event on Facebook with a picture teaser and share it widely. Tweet about it. Ask your local newspaper to cover the event. Get local bookstores involved by putting up a poster near an eye-catching display of Sendak's book.

Variations

❭ *Host a StoryWalk.* See the sidebar for more information.
❭ *A Tintamarre.* Celebrate National Acadian Day (August 15 in Canada) by throwing this traditional party and parade.[12]

Materials Required

❏ Refreshments: water, Freezies, Popsicles, goldfish crackers, green grapes, Bugles, and carrot sticks
❏ Napkins or baby wipes
❏ Garbage can
❏ Noisemakers
❏ Hula hoops
❏ Fabric
❏ Yellow cardstock and markers, glitter, fake gems, feathers, and other things to decorate crowns with
❏ Empty boxes

Anne Ferguson

Name: Anne Ferguson, retired Chronic Disease Prevention Specialist

Contact: storywalkvt@yahoo.com

Location: Kellogg-Hubbard Library, Montpelier, Vermont

Claim to Fame: StoryWalk Project Founder

All-Star Program: The StoryWalk Project

A child enjoying a StoryWalk

When I created the StoryWalk Project in 2007, I knew I had a great idea; I just didn't anticipate how well it would be received across the country and beyond. The idea was quite simple: take the pages from a children's picture book, attach each one to a stake, and line them up along a path for folks to read and enjoy.

One of my supervisors told me that the secret to promoting a health message was "partners, partners, partners," and as many and varied partners as possible. I was working as a chronic disease prevention specialist at the time, and I knew that I wanted to create something different, fun, and interesting. I had tried some different approaches involving children, but I found that the parents stood around chatting while the children were physically active. I knew I wanted to create something where the parents had to be as active as the children. Active parents have active children, and physical activity is a key component in chronic disease prevention.

In order to keep people of all ages moving along on a walk, I knew I needed books with minimal text that would appeal to all ages (especially children) and that could fit into families' busy schedules. I wanted my project to be free so financial limits would not interfere with people enjoying it. I fleetingly thought about writing a children's book myself, but I knew that there were already many marvelous, funny, beautiful, and moving stories available.

I wanted to use existing books, but I didn't know about the legalities of doing that. I made some calls and found out that if the book is used without altering the text or the page in any way (shrinking, copying, or enlarging the pages), I could use it without needing to ask for permission.

I had no money and no staff for this idea, so I knew it would have to be self-generated. I contacted the early literacy person at the Vermont Arts Council, who immediately gave me $250 to start the project. My employer gave me one month to try it. I purchased David Ezra Stein's book *Leaves* and started preparing it for posting. I selected the most popular path in our local park and put out a notebook for feedback.

The response was tremendous and positive. Unfortunately, my employer told me I couldn't continue focusing on StoryWalk. So I went ahead with it on my own time. I applied for and got a grant so I could purchase more books, lamination, and stakes.

I learned a lot about how to prepare the books for posting. I learned that I needed to number the pages on the back to ensure that they were posted in the correct order; I learned that it is best to use Velcro on the stakes and the book pages; and I learned that I could loan the StoryWalk books out through my partner, the Kellogg-Hubbard Library. I learned that the partners in my community that were interested in this project included state and local parks, schools, nature centers, child care centers, farmers markets, walking path promoters, special event promotions, and most of all, libraries.

Through the Kellogg-Hubbard Library in my home town of Montpelier, Vermont, I have loaned out the StoryWalk books at no charge to borrowers from all over the state of Vermont. I keep the books stored in a barn that is located between my house and the library. I am the scheduler for all of the books. All borrowers pick up and return the books to the library. All borrowers receive a contract that they need to sign saying that they will care for the book and pay for any damage to it.

Vandals are a recurring challenge. They seem to be threatened by a story about Gossie, a small duck who has misplaced his red rubber boots. A range of approaches has been used to address this issue, some with greater success than others. The Velcro makes it easy to take down the pages before dark and post them again in the morning. Vandals prefer the cover of darkness.

My partnership with the Kellogg-Hubbard Library has been instrumental in spreading the word about the StoryWalk Project. The library provides a link on its website to StoryWalk where people can learn more about how to bring the project to their community, and Vermonters can find out what books are offered and how to arrange to borrow them.

continued on the following page ❱❱❱

continued from the previous page 〉〉〉

StoryWalk was never designed to be a money-making project. In fact, it is now supported solely by donations from the public. It has always been about promoting early literacy, physical activity, and family time spent together in nature. Its success is due to partners, partners, partners that understood from the beginning how this idea could be used to bring a fun and educational family activity to their community. That is why in the 10 years since I created StoryWalk, it has spread to (at the last count) all 50 states and 12 foreign countries. People everywhere are encouraged to bring it to their community. You can learn more by reading the FAQ about StoryWalk which can be accessed through my greatest partner, the Kellogg-Hubbard Library, at their website.[13] Without the support of the library and, in particular, Rachel Senechal, program director and development coordinator, this project would not be as well-known and widespread as it is today.

- ❏ *Where the Wild Things Are* by Maurice Sendak
- ❏ Large Lego bricks/blocks
- ❏ Portable stereo, Bluetooth speaker and device, or laptop and speakers
- ❏ Liability waivers
- ❏ Photo release forms and camera (if using)
- ❏ Parent evaluation forms (if using)
- ❏ Music

    Sample Playlist:
    - ◦ *Rumpus*, by Karen O and the Kids (from *Where the Wild Things Are* soundtrack)
    - ◦ *Monster Mash*, by Bobby Pickett
    - ◦ *Wild Thing*, by The Troggs
    - ◦ *Born to Be Wild*, by Steppenwolf
    - ◦ *What Does the Fox Say*, by Ylvis

Budget Details

$20–50

We gathered large sheets of fabric, hula hoops, giant Lego blocks, and empty cardboard boxes from our existing stash and got more empty boxes from the local Walmart and liquor store. The yellow cardstock and craft supplies for the crowns will cost about $10–20. Refreshments will cost $10+, depending on what you serve and how many people attend.

Day of Event

STEP 1. Gather all needed supplies and set up your activity room to make the crowns.

STEP 2. Greet everyone as they arrive and have the parents or guardians sign liability waivers.

STEP 3. Have each participant craft their own paper crown to match Max's crown in the book, or let them freestyle it.

STEP 4. Have a half an hour of free play and dance. This time can be shortened or extended depending on the age ranges and the group size.

STEP 5. Once all participants have had ample time to play and create, read *Where the Wild Things Are.*

STEP 6. Play *Rumpus* by Karen O and the Kids and jangle noisemakers all the way through the library for a Wild Walk. Dance as you go and try out different walking techniques. Outdoors works too, especially if your other library patrons (or staff) get cranky about "excessive noise."

STEP 7. Have a quick snack.

STEP 8. Hand out evaluations and while you are snacking, talk with all of the participants about what they liked about the event.

Tips

1. Consider adding some special guests to the event. Perhaps a local celebrity to read the book or someone dressed in a Max costume to lead the parade.

2. This program can be condensed to fit into a thirty-minute storytime by removing some of the activities, or it could be extended into an entire afternoon by adding on; you choose!

3. Try this program out with a group of teens or preteens; you might be surprised how much fun they have.

Multiple Literacy Tie-In

❱ Create a cool display of monster-related books to encourage families to take the fun home with them. Don't forget to include multiple formats (audiobooks, braille, kits, etc.). Here are some good ones to get you started:

° *Go Away, Big Green Monster!* by Ed Emberley
° *Goodnight Goon: A Petrifying Parody,* by Michael Rex

- *If You're a Monster and You Know It,* by Rebecca Emberley and Ed Emberley
- *Leonardo, the Terrible Monster,* by Mo Willems
- *The Monster at the End of This Book: Starring Lovable, Furry Old Grover,* by Jon Stone
- *Monster Mess!* by Margery Cuyler
- *Monsters Don't Eat Broccoli,* by Barbara Jean Hicks
- *My Monster Mama Loves Me So,* by Laura Leuck
- *The Very Worst Monster,* by Pat Hutchins

PROGRAM MODEL
Family Yoga Class

A Family Yoga Class is a great opportunity to introduce people of all ages to yoga in a low-pressure environment. Watching parents and guardians try to touch their toes will give kids the giggles, and the class gives everyone some take-home mindfulness tools to use in their daily lives. June 21 is International Yoga Day, but you don't have to wait until June to celebrate; you can have a Family Yoga Class any day of the year you want.[14]

FIGURE 4.15
Family Yoga poster

Advance Planning

STEP 1. Pick a date and time for the event. During the day works for stay-home or shift-work families, day cares, and the after-school crowd. Evenings might work, but you have to remember that a lot of children are in scheduled weekly activities in the evenings, especially during the school year. Weekend mornings or afternoons are often good times for families. I recommend having pre-registration so you know how many mats you will need. Decide how long the program will last. A duration of 30–45 minutes is best; if the class is too long, the youngest will get antsy.

STEP 2. Figure out your best location: an activity room, the library's front lawn, the children's department. A suitable place is anywhere you have a big open area in which you can put down some mats.

STEP 3. Find an instructor. The best-case scenario is having someone on staff who is already a certified yoga teacher (minimum 200 hours of training),

FIGURE 4.16 Family Yoga

but you may be able to use a volunteer. Contact your local yoga studios, meditation centers, or gyms to see if anyone would mind volunteering their time. Local yoga Facebook groups are also good places to look. Make sure the teacher has liability insurance. Usually staff members leading a class inside the library during working hours are covered under your library's existing insurance plan (check with your administration to be sure), but outside instructors might need their own insurance, just to be safe. If you can't get a volunteer, you can usually hire an instructor for $20–100 per hour, depending on the class size and their years of experience. Sometimes new teachers who are almost done with their training will need to log a number of practicum hours, so this might be a good fit. If you can't find a certified instructor, you could lead the class yourself, if you feel comfortable. If you need some ideas of poses to do in your own Family Yoga Class, check out the class videos or books on my website www.yogainthelibrary.com, or read Kate Scherrer's super-helpful *Stories, Songs, and Stretches! Creating Playful Storytimes with Yoga and Movement.* You can check her out in the Activity All-Star sidebar.

STEP 4. Advertise. Make a poster, put it on your event calendar and website, make a Facebook event, and don't forget word of mouth. An enthusiastic Summer Reading Club Leader can promote the class to members during regularly scheduled SRC events if it is held in the summer.

FIGURE 4.17 Family Yoga coloring

STEP 5. Create liability waivers and photo release forms if you plan on taking pictures or video for use on your library's website or Facebook page.

STEP 6. Secure enough mats for all participants; either the instructor can bring them along, or you can ask people to bring their own, or you can buy some. Beanbags are useful too, for centering the breath.

Variations

❭ *Family Yoga Triathlon.* This consists of a one-mile run/walk, a 30-minute family-style yoga class, and a 10-minute group meditation.

❭ *Family Meditation Session.* These have been really popular at my library. There are some great books for teaching meditation and mindfulness techniques to kids. A great activity is one in which the whole family sits in a circle and holds hands and silently thinks to themselves: "I love Daddy because. . . . , I love my sister because. . . ." Everyone goes around the circle thinking about the reasons why they care about their family members. This usually results in lots of hugs and tears at the end.

❭ *Bilingual Yoga Storytime.* See the sidebar for more information.

Materials Required

❏ Liability waivers

❏ Evaluation forms (if using)

❏ Photo release forms and camera (if using)

❏ Music and device to play it on (if using)

❏ Yoga mats

❏ Beanbags

❏ Bell or singing bowl

Budget Details

$0–200+

Finding a volunteer instructor (or someone on staff with existing training) who can provide all the mats and props means that you have won the lottery. So that's probably not going to happen (but it does—I've seen it). But don't fret—there are many grants you can apply for that will help pay for sporting equipment to be used by nonprofits. Don't hesitate to think outside the box by requesting funding from wellness or mental health-centered organizations. Local sporting goods stores may also be willing to sponsor your program provided you credit them in your marketing materials. If you are a certified instructor, you are also eligible for discounts if you order wholesale from Halfmoon Yoga Products[15] or Lululemon.[16] Never underestimate the power of yogis to be awesome philanthropists—I've had much success with approaching local yoga-loving business people and asking them to write me checks to buy supplies. If you can't find a volunteer or student who needs their teaching hours, hiring a teacher is going to cost you between $20 and $150 an hour depending on their experience and local demand. A singing bowl, which is also known as a standing bell, is going to run you about $30 or more, depending on the size. These bowls are struck with a wooden mallet—which can also be rotated around the rim to sustain a note—and are widely used to create a vibrational shift that can clear thought-patterns. You can always pilfer a xylophone from the children's department instead, it will certainly get the children's attention.

Day of the Event

STEP 1. Set up the mats, singing bowl, and props and test the music (if you are using).

Katie Scherrer

Name: Katie Scherrer, Library Consultant, Yoga Teacher

Contact: katie@connectedcommunitiesconsulting.com

Location: Lexington, Kentucky

Claim to Fame: *Stories, Songs, and Stretches! Creating Playful Storytimes with Yoga and Movement* and *Once Upon a Cuento: Bilingual Storytimes in English and Spanish* (coauthored with Jamie Campbell Naidoo)

All-Star Program: ¡Yoguitos! Bilingual Yoga Storytime Fun

This is a playful bilingual storytime for families. Take this program on the road as part of your outreach efforts to Latino and Spanish-speaking families to show how active and fun storytimes can be, in addition to helping prepare children for school. Use books and music by Latino authors, illustrators, and artists to highlight the diverse collection your library has available. This program plan can be modified to accommodate monolingual Spanish storytimes and mostly English storytimes.

Book: *Julieta y un día en el jardín: Un cuento de primavera de yoga para niños* by Giselle Shardlow, illustrated by Hazel Quintanilla. Available in English as *Rachel's Day in the Garden: A Kids Yoga Spring Colors Book*.

Explore the colors of spring as you make various yoga shapes. Poses and simple instructions are included in the story and featured in the illustrations.

Song: "Muévete" from *From Here to There* by Nathalia.

This is a fun bilingual song that will have everyone clapping, spinning, and jumping along.

STEP 2. Don't forget the waivers and photo releases (if using), and either set up a table at the door to make sure every family signs or have a clipboard for when they arrive.

STEP 3. Class time! Here's a sample class idea:

❭ Introduction and rules (return to your mat and sit crisscross-applesauce whenever you hear the bell, keep your hands to yourself, and only do what feels good for your body).

Book: *Call Me Tree / Llámame árbol* by Maya Christina Gonzalez.

Grow from a seed to a tree along with many diverse children as you read this bilingual book.

Movement: La cicla de vida de un árbol / Tree Life Cycle

Act out the life cycle of a tree with the following yoga poses or movements. Use a flannelboard, pictures, or digital tools to incorporate a visual element.

English Term	Término en español	Yoga Pose or Movement
seed	la semilla	child's pose
roots	las raices	wide-leg seated pose
sprout	el brote	hero pose
rain	la lluvia	tap on legs while seated
sun	el sol	high kneeling with arms overhead in circle
tree	el árbol	tree pose

Book: *Gracias / Thanks* by Pat Mora, illustrated by John Parra.

Take a moment to pause and experience gratitude for the simple joys in life with this lovely story.

Rest

As a group, lie down in any way that is comfortable for one to two minutes of quiet rest.

Closing Song: "De Colores"

This traditional folk song, well known by many Latinos and Spanish-speakers from around the world, celebrates love and the beauty of the natural world. Many recordings are available. Jose-Luis Orozco's version from *De Colores and Other Latin American Folk Songs for Children* is highly recommended.

❭ Conduct three rounds of the "Rainbow Power Song," which I learned from Leah Kalish (Sun Salutation A). Each posture of a sun salutation is given a color of the rainbow. You can find a video of this sequence at www.yogainthelibrary.com under the "digital resources" page.

❭ Play the "felt square on head" partner game (try and pass a felt square back and forth—with no hands).

❭ Finger plays: "Hands in the Air" and "Worm" by Kevin MacKenzie.

> Postures: flowerpot, star (while singing "Twinkle, Twinkle Little Star"), donkey, coyote, cat-cow, dog, lion.

> Truck race game (pretend to be trucks and "drive" from one end of the room to the other).

> Read *Trucks Go* by Steve Light.

> Closing remarks.

> Coloring page to do in class or to take home, depending on the parent or teacher's schedule.

STEP 4. Clean up and hand out evaluations, if using.

Tips

1. If you can't find or afford a professional teacher and you don't feel comfortable teaching, but you still would like to add some yoga or movement to an existing program, check out www.GoNoodle.com, a website of free videos for educators that get kids moving.

2. Don't worry about all the different ages mixed together. The younger children will feel more comfortable taking risks and learning from the examples set by the older children, and the older children will learn the responsibility of teaching, modeling, and caretaking by having the younger ones around.[17]

3. Don't take talking during the class to mean they aren't interested. Remember, for a lot of parents, this might be their only opportunity that day to have another adult to chat with, and they relish the chance for connection. A quick two- or three-question survey at the end of the class would also be a great way to measure their engagement, but don't take it personally if they rush out and don't complete it; they have a mini-person who needs their immediate attention, or they have appointments they can't miss. Take nothing personally.

4. Don't use wordy instructions. Use short, clear, concise directions and lots of demonstrating. Kids will mirror your behavior. Instead of saying, "Let's do the butterfly pose. First you sit down with your feet touching and your knees out to the sides. Then you hold your feet. Then you take a nice deep inhale and lean over your toes . . . ," try doing the pose while saying, "Let's be butterflies! Flap your wings (knees up and down) and smell the flowers (lean forward and breathe deep)!"

5. Modulate your voice and energy to help keep control of theirs. If they are manic and bouncing off the walls, get their attention by clapping and singing a little song, getting softer and quieter. They'll simmer down so they can hear you and follow along. Try "I'm a Little Teapot" with the actions, and when you get to the "pour me out" part, everyone collapses to the floor. If they are sluggish and you are losing them, bump up the volume of your voice and get more animated. A classic like "Twinkle, Twinkle, Little Star" while making a standing star shape and rocking back and forth from foot to foot works every time. Or you can bust out your inner ballerina like The Wiggles (musical act, for the uninitiated). Finger plays are always attention-grabbers. Kevin MacKenzie has some great free ones you can watch on his website.[18]

6. Remember to play and not take yourself seriously. Play is the work of childhood, and children play to learn how to exercise control over their environment and themselves. Learn from them. As Joseph Chilton Pearce says, "There are no big or little events to the two-year-old, all is breathless excitement, awe and wonder."[19]

7. If you've got a crowd who is a bit older, read the sweet and bright book *The Color Monster: A Pop-Up Book of Feelings* by Anna Llenas (available in Spanish and French too) and talk about how it is possible to feel many different feelings at once. We can discover that we are not our feelings, but we can learn about them and see what they have to teach us about ourselves. We can practice naming the feelings and assigning them a color and acting them out. Then for the coloring page, provide a gender-neutral outline of a human for the children to color with whatever colors they are feeling right then. This ties in well with the words from the "Rainbow Power Song."

8. Follow their lead. Think of the class as "guided play." Don't be afraid to switch gears if something isn't working. Always have a backup plan. This might be a "follow-the-train" through the stacks in the children's department, or it might be ending early and doing an impromptu craft. Have reasonable expectations. Don't use formal breathing exercises. Don't focus on alignment. Keep that inner control freak in check. If they aren't getting your swan pose, just roll around on the floor and giggle. Don't worry about the parents watching on the sidelines who aren't joining in. Most of them are just happy their child is being entertained, and they are probably playing on their cell phones anyway.

Multiple Literacy Tie-In

❫ There are many great books and DVDs on the market about yoga and movement, but there are also some that are not so great. Make a display for participants to browse and take home afterwards. Here's some popular choices, and you can find in-depth reviews and more titles at www.yogainthelibrary.com.

❫ Display of educational DVDs that are family-friendly:

- *Elmosize* (2006)
- *Fingersplay: Finger Plays and Action Rhymes for Children* (2002)
- *Storyland Yoga: Yoga for Kids and Families* (2010)
- *Time to Play* (2014)
- *Yoga for Families: Connect with Your Kids* (2009)
- *Yoga Kids* (2010)

❫ Display of yoga books geared towards families. These are some of my favorites. I review more on www.yogainthelibrary.com:

- *Children's Book of Yoga: Games & Exercises Mimic Plants & Animals & Objects,* by Thia Luby
- *Fly Like a Butterfly: Yoga for Children,* by Shakata K. Khalsa
- *Once Upon a Pose: A Guide to Yoga Adventure Stories for Children,* by Donna Freeman
- *The Treasure in Your Heart: Stories and Yoga for Peaceful Children,* by Sydney Solis and Melanie Sumner
- *Yoga for Children: 200+ Yoga Poses, Breathing Exercises, and Meditations for Healthier, Happier, More Resilient Children,* by Lisa Flynn
- *Yoga for Kids,* by Liz Lark
- *Yoga for You & Your Child: The Step-by-Step Guide to Enjoying Yoga with Children of All Ages,* by Mark Singleton

PROGRAM MODEL
Water Games Party

At the height of the Summer Reading Club (or during an autumn back-to-school heat wave), sometimes the best thing to do is take the kids outside and hose them down—that will get the fidgets out! (Just kidding.) But seriously, throwing water balloons at people or targets IS extremely therapeutic. This program is also a great way to improve physical literacy skills, such as jumping, running, aiming, throwing, carrying, squeezing, and catching . . . while also improving social skills through teamwork. With all the measuring and counting games, we're also improving our math and physics knowledge. And we make art, by filling water guns with paint! This program is perfect for those working in the low-to-no budget zone (collective sigh—how awesome would it be if we could afford giant Nerf Super Soakers for everyone?). Even if the sky is threatening rain, this program is a crowd-pleaser, leaving the kids (and their parents) begging for more.

FIGURE 4.18
Water Games poster

Advance Planning

STEP 1. Pick a date and time for the event. Keep in mind that the participants will go home wet, unless they bring a change of clothes. During summer vacation, any afternoon or weekend might work. During the school year, later in the afternoon might work, or the weekend. Pre-registration is helpful so you have an idea of how much supplies to prepare ahead of time. Decide how long the program will last. Depending on the age of the participants and how many games you prepare, this could be a thirty-minute program or it could last for hours.

STEP 2. Figure out your best location: a local park, the library's front lawn, a nearby field. A suitable location is anywhere you have a big open area that is safe from traffic. We are a downtown library with very little nearby green space, so we just cordoned off a section of the parking lot.

FIGURE 4.19 Water painting

STEP 3. Advertise. Make a poster, put it on your event calendar and website, make a Facebook event, and don't forget word of mouth. An enthusiastic Summer Reading Club Leader can promote the program to members during regularly scheduled SRC events if it is held in the summer. A fun way to get kids enthusiastic (and save yourself some work filling so many water balloons) is to make little flyers with an attached balloon and either give them out during the SRC or when families pre-register and tell them to bring the balloon back filled with water and prepared to do battle! You (or they) could even write or draw something on the balloon with a sharpie.

STEP 4. Create liability waivers and photo release forms if you plan on taking pictures or video for use on your library's website or Facebook page.

STEP 5. Plan your games.[20] Depending on the age of your expected crowd, you can make them simple or more complicated. This program also works really well with teens. You can decide whether you want to have prizes for the games or not; we don't use any (it keeps costs down and encourages a more process-oriented environment rather than a reward-based one).

》 *Duck Duck Goose:* This is played like a regular game of Duck Duck Goose but is more menacing! Players sit in a circle and the person who is "it" goes around tapping everyone on the head saying "duck, duck, duck . . ." until they pick a new person to be the "Goose!" by breaking a water balloon over the person's head.

FIGURE 4.20 Sponge Bucket Relay

❭ *Sponge Bucket Relay:* In this game, participants are divided into two equal teams and line up on one side of the play area. Each team has an empty bucket and a sponge. They have to take turns racing to a big bucket filled with water on the other side of the play area, soaking their sponge with water, and then carefully carrying it back and squeezing out the water into their empty bucket by wringing out the sponge. The teammates waiting at the home bucket cheer on the person running to fill up the sponge, who then trades off with the next player. If you have enough sponges and buckets, you could have more than two teams. For added difficulty, you could ask the groups to try to make an object in the empty bucket float. The first team to transfer enough water—to either float the object or reach the high-water line drawn on the bucket—wins.

❭ *Water Balloon Toss:* In pairs, participants stand across from each other, starting very close together. They pass a water balloon back and forth between them without the balloon breaking. After each toss, participants each take a step away from each other. If they break their balloon, they have to return to their starting distance. Whichever team gets to the long-distance marker first wins.

❭ *Water Gun Painting:* Using cheap water guns from the dollar store, each participant helps paint a piece of art for the library to display. Buy as many canvases as you want to display, or else you could buy small canvases and each family could take one home, but we like to get one or two really big ones to display in the children's department—it looks super cool with drippy paint splatters! Dilute some poster paint in water in a Ziploc bag, and then cut a small corner off the bag and squeeze the solution into the water gun. You might want to test it first to see if it is dark enough. Have one gun for each paint color. Each patron takes turns shooting the canvases with their chosen paint color. Canvases can also be spun around to mix the colors. Parents will really enjoy this activity, especially since it gives them a break from being pelted with water balloons!

❭ *Water Fight:* This is a free-for-all water balloon fight. Either everyone gets a certain allotment of balloons, or there is a large tote filled with balloons that everyone can grab from at their own peril because someone will inevitably stand guard and get them as they come in for supplies. In order to reduce the risk of injury, I recommend no shots above the neck.

❭ *Target Practice:* If you have enough water guns and the space, set up targets at one end of the play area and people can practice their skills during downtime or if there is a game they don't feel like participating in.

❭ *Fishing Game:* Set up a tiny inflatable pool, fill it with water, and supply a magnetic fishing game which the kids can play with while waiting for the next activity to begin. This is also a pleasant distraction for very young children while their big siblings take part in the more rowdy and competitive play.

❭ *Cold Potato:* Have participants sit or stand in a circle. A water balloon is the "potato." Have kids pass the balloon to the person beside them going as fast as they can. If a player fails to catch the balloon and it breaks, they are "out." If a player intentionally throws the balloon too hard and it breaks when it hits the next person, they are "out." The game goes until there is only one person left. One variation to add difficulty is to have the players take a step backwards on each round.

❭ *Ice Race:* Give everyone an ice cube and see who can melt theirs the fastest. Try different techniques (putting it in one's mouth, in the sun, in water, on skin, on grass, on one's head, etc.).

STEP 6. Buy or borrow your supplies. See the "Materials Required" section for a list of possibilities. Make ice if you need to.

Variations

⟩ **Water Wars!** Design the program to target a teen audience with a more competitive edge. Buy or borrow giant water guns if you can and play a modified version of Capture the Flag (see "Nerf Battle" in chapter 5 for more inspiration). If you have access to a garden hose, try playing water limbo!

⟩ **Splish Splash Preschool Bash.** Invite parents and their children ages 3–5 for an exciting sensory immersion. Fill different tubs and buckets with water and floaties and let the kids play freely. Have lots of cups and scoops so they can practice pouring, and provide sponges so they can practice squeezing. They can try rolling, squishing, tossing, and bouncing water balloons (be careful they don't put any broken pieces in their mouths). Ice cubes and bubbles are also great to play with. If it is very warm and you have a grassy play area, it might be fun to put out a sprinkler or small inflatable pool, but remember that the grass around it will become slippery. You can try one or two organized games, but at this age free play and exploration are best.

Materials Required

❑ A least a few packs of water balloons—there's a brand called "Bunch O Balloons" that are self-sealing and you can fill many at once. They are available at our local Walmart store and come in packs of 100. This brand cannot be filled up too far in advance because they leak water over time.

❑ Something to store all your ready-to-go balloons in (garbage can, tote, wagon, or a box that you don't mind getting wet).

❑ Large sponges (make sure they are the same size).

❑ At least four buckets (you can use storage totes you already have as long as they are the same size).

❑ Water.

❑ Floating objects (ping-pong balls work well).

❑ Water guns.

❑ Poster paint.

❑ Blank canvases.

❑ Ziploc bags.

❑ Magnetic fishing kit.

❏ Small inflatable pool (you could also use a large dishpan or tote if you have one).

❏ Caution tape (for sectioning off the parking lot—if you have a big lawn or park available, that's even better—we're downtown, so use what you've got).

❏ Junk for targets—old CDs hanging off string, old posters with bulls-eyes drawn on them, empty cans from the recycling bin—get creative!

❏ Liability waivers, photo releases, and evaluation forms (if using).

❏ Ice (make it or buy a bag—but make sure it is safe to consume).

❏ Water hose/sprinkler (if using).

Budget Details

$10–50+

You could keep this program really low-cost by only playing games that require balloons and/or using existing items you already own for the other games. If you have to pay a municipal water bill, keep that in mind before you face a cranky table of board members. The small pool and magnetic fishing game will cost you $10–20, depending on the size of the pool.

Day of the Event

STEP 1. Fill up the water balloons. You may want to recruit volunteers for this. Wear clothes that you feel comfortable being wet in. You will probably be covered in water before the kids even arrive.

STEP 2. Get out all the other props and prepare the play area.

STEP 3. Prepare liability waivers and photo releases (if using) on a clipboard and have them ready for parents to sign.

STEP 4. Put out refreshments (if you are providing some) and extra sunscreen and towels for those who may have forgotten.

STEP 5. As participants arrive, have them try out the inflatable pool or target practice while they wait. Once everyone is there, go over the rules.

STEP 6. Play whichever games you've chosen and have a great time.

STEP 7. Ask everyone to go on a scavenger hunt to find broken pieces of balloon. Make sure no garbage is left behind.

STEP 8. Hand out evaluation forms, if using.

STEP 9. Put away everything and towel off. High-five yourself and colleagues for having an awesome event.

Tips

1. Obviously, you need to keep an eye on the weather, but don't feel you need to cancel just because it is raining (thunder and lightning or high winds? yes). You are going to be wet anyway, and playing in warm rain adds a fun element to the games (though you might want to reconsider the water art). We've had a very good turnout even on an overcast day.

2. You will get obscenely wet. Kids love throwing water balloons at librarians and teachers. Wear something appropriate. Today might not be the day for your best white T-shirt or pants, unless you are having an adult-only, after-hours water party. That would be the subject of a *very* different book. Try to stay within your company dress code and bring something to change into afterwards. You may also want a towel and hair dryer (and possibly makeup remover and new makeup if you wear it), unless that caught-in-the-rain look is what you were going for today.

3. Think about footwear. Participants may want to be barefoot, unless you are in a gravel parking lot or litter-filled lot. Establish rules ahead of time.

4. Be careful of people wearing glasses. They may wish to remove them or else not have any water balloons broken on their head. Ask first. Making "no shots above the neck" is also a good rule (except for playing Duck Duck Goose).

5. You might want to provide drinks if it is hot out, or ask participants to bring water bottles. Make sure to remind everyone to put on sunscreen.

6. Remind participants to bring a change of clothes and/or towels. You might want to have a couple of old towels on hand so dripping wet kids who need to use the bathroom don't slip and fall on the library's floor.

7. You will always need more water balloons than you think you will. Buy 100 percent more than you originally planned. If your eco-warrior insides are cringing at the thought of all those broken balloons and wasted rubber/latex, you can always buy biodegradable balloons, but they will be much pricier.[21]

8. This program is easily adaptable/inclusive for those with mobility issues. Someone who has obvious difficulty walking or running could be assigned as the "keeper of the balloons" and can defend the stronghold, but make sure to ask them first—they may want to just join in the melee. Let them lead. Targets can be adjusted for various heights. Sponges can be squeezed even by people with limited manual dexterity. With such a wide range of ages (preschoolers to adults), everyone will be soaking wet and howling with laughter, regardless of ability.

9. Be mindful that many of the kids and parents might be wearing bathing suits, and they might not feel comfortable having their, or their child's, picture taken. It's always better to ask.

Multiple Literacy Tie-In

Here are some display ideas or activities to expand your program offerings.

❱ A display of juvenile-friendly materials on water, oceans, and water sports. For example:

- *Coral Reefs: Cities of the Ocean*, by Maris Wicks
- *Dino-Swimming*, by Lisa Wheeler
- *Newborn Floating to Toddler Swimming*, by Francoise Barbira-Freedman
- *Ocean Animals*, by Garry Fleming
- *Ocean by Miranda*, by MacQuitty
- *The 100 Best Swimming Drills*, by Lucero Blythe
- *Peppa Goes Swimming*, by Mark Baker
- *Sailing Alone around the World*, by Joshua Slocum
- *Surfing: A Beginner's Guide*, by Alf Alderson
- *Surfing: An Illustrated History of the Coolest Sport of All Time*, by Ben Marcus
- *Swimming and Diving*, by Clive Gifford
- *Water*, by Ellen Lawrence
- *Water*, by Geoff Havel
- Water Babies: Safe Starts in Swimming: Teach Your Baby the Joys of Water—From *Water Polo Is Fun*, by John Craig
- *Water Sports*, by Bob Woods
- *Water, Water*, by Eloise Greenfield and Jan Spivey Gilchrist
- *White Water*, by Jonathon London, Aaron London, and Jill Kastner

❱ Incorporate a mini-lesson about the properties of water and how 50–60 percent of our body is made of water. You could even have a slide of water under a microscope to look at, or check out the pictures in *The Hidden Messages in Water* by Masaru Emoto, or check out his other books. With middle-schoolers or teens, you can talk about the science and philosophy behind how what we think/feel and the experiences we have affect our bodies on a molecular level.

❱ Give free passes to a local swimming pool or water park. Ask your recreation department or local water attractions if they would be willing to partner with you, and you can use these passes as prizes, or else as part of an alternative collection as a "checkout" item.

⟩ Create a map of all the local water attractions in your area to hand out at the information desk and during the event. If you live in an area near a famous body of water, you could incorporate a display of items about that river, lake, ocean, or waterfall. For example, Woodstock is at the place where the Meduxnekeag River flows into the St. John River, and we have books about both bodies of water. We are also a few minutes away from Hays Falls on the Maliseet trail (part of a famous Indigenous portage route), so we can add information about that to the display.

Notes

1. Miriam P. Trehearne, *Multiple Paths to Literacy: Proven High-Yield Strategies to Scaffold Emerging Literacy Learning across the Curriculum* (Calgary, AB: Miriam P. Trehearne Literacy Consulting, 2016).

2. Angela Hanscom, *Balanced and Barefoot: How Unrestricted Outdoor Play Makes for Strong, Confident, and Capable Children* (Oakland, CA: New Harbinger, 2016).

3. Canadian Sport Tourism Alliance, "Sport Tourism Surges Past $6.5 Billion Annually," Canadian Sport Tourism Alliance News, 2017, http://canadiansporttourism.com/news/sport-tourism-surges-past-65-billion-annually.html; National Association of Sports Commissions, "National Association of Sports Commissions Releases Annual State of the Industry Report," 2017, https://www.sportscommissions.org/Blog/article/ID/738/National-Association-of-Sports-Commissions-Releases-Annual-State-of-the-Industry-Report.

4. Playlist compiled by Ebony Scott.

5. See SOCAN's website for more information in Canada: https://www.socan.ca/licensees/faq-licensing.

6. Super Simple Online, "Super Simple Songs," https://supersimpleonline.com/super-simple-songs/ and The Learning Groove www.thelearninggroove.com are excellent resources.

7. The whole playlist can be found at https://www.youtube.com/playlist?list=PLL4f1_NK3NuRaoBsYdAzSka100jq8hy6Z.

8. We're not the first library to hold a Wild Rumpus; we borrowed some ideas from the Madison Public Library: http://librarymakers.blogspot.ca/2016/06/let-wild-rumpus-start.html.

9. Google "crown template" to save you trying to draw one yourself.

10. If this doesn't appeal to you or you are short on paper tubes, Google "noise maker crafts" for many other good ideas.

11. Triangle-shaped corn chips, for the uninitiated.

12. Learn more about the history of the Tintamarre here: www.ameriquefrancaise.org/en/article-319/Tintamarre:_a_New_Acadian_%E2%80%9CTradition%E2%80%9D_.html.

13. Kellogg-Hubbard Library, "StoryWalk," www.kellogghubbard.org/storywalk.

14. Yoga Day was first made official by the United Nations on December 11, 2014.

15. Halfmoon, "Wholesale," https://www.shophalfmoon.com/wholesale.

16. Lululemon, "Wholesale," https://info.lululemon.com/about/strategic-sales/wholesale.

17. Hanscom, *Balanced and Barefoot*.

18. Kevin MacKenzie, "Fingerplays!" Stories by Kevin, www.storiesbykevin.com/fingersplay.html.

19. Joseph Chilton Pearce, *Magical Child* (New York: Plume, 1992).

20. Special thanks to Ebony Scott for her creativity in coming up with some of these games.

21. They cost about $20 for 100 balloons the last time I checked on Amazon.com.

5

Energy in Motion
Helping Teens Self-Regulate through Movement

All adolescents are saturated with new hormones, new and acute kinds of self-consciousness, new kinds of desires, and confronted with the avalanche of new responsibilities that are associated with the threshold of adulthood. All of this physical and mental turmoil creates a new kind of muscular tension in the adolescent. They squirm. They chew their fingernails. They tap their feet. They screw themselves up into the damndest kind of postures. They jump up and down and shout at the slightest provocation. They are like tightly wound springs.

—*Deane Juhan, Job's Body: A Handbook for Bodywork*

It's a real tragedy that in some public libraries, teen programming tends to get lumped in with children's programming, or else neglected altogether, because this demographic is badly in need of connection. I mean, I get the whole avoidance issue from our end, they aren't exactly a low-hanging fruit; the teens in my town mostly come in to use the computers, use the bathroom, and hang out. Some of them actually read books. Most of them wouldn't be caught dead participating in a group event and looking like they were having fun while doing it. Today's teens are so busy with sports, school, clubs, friends, volunteering, working, their smartphones, and a million other things that we have to be truly innovative to get them in the activity-room doors. I had to learn this trial-by-fire style when I was given a one-year contract to run the Hampton High School Library while their librarian was on leave. The library was a dead zone. Like, crickets, except for my squeaky book truck and a few socially withdrawn students who hung out in the library at lunch, escaping from the noise in the halls to read alone, or work on their homework, or occasionally play *Magic: The Gathering* with each other. I had no previous relationship with the students or staff, so I had to figure out how to get people to trust me while also selling them on the idea that the library was more than a computer lab (which it also was). The most social interaction I had was from teachers coming in to use the photocopier and laminator and make small talk over the smell of toner and melting plastic. The library, to my knowledge, had never had any programs other than a yearly introductory tour for each grade and the occasional teacher-led class visit.

So I started with what I knew best, teaching yoga classes at noon and after school, which were well-attended, but I knew I needed to do more. I wasn't reaching the kids who needed the activity and interaction the most. I decided to create the HHS Library Guild.[1] At first it was mostly to entertain me and find a way to engage with my few off-the-beat regulars. These teens were what would have been called "misfits" in my day: stereotypically nerdy, or supremely shy, or wearing the "wrong" clothes, or aggressively opinionated, or openly, unrepentantly sexually subversive, or angry and misunderstood, or all of the above. Some of them had diagnosed conditions that were known to me. Others were publicly label-less, but they were still very aware they didn't belong in the halls with the *cool* kids. I got it. I had never been particularly popular either, and I was/am definitely odd. I hung out at the library so much as a kid that I made it into a profession. I knew these teens were harboring some very real skills and hidden awesomeness; it just needed a safe space to come out. And they were a very sedentary bunch. We're not talking about a high degree of physical literacy here. They were *not* the ones coming to my yoga classes. These were not the kids who were picked first in gym class. We needed to get moving.

So, again, I did what I knew how to do. First, I got interested in what they were interested in. I asked, I listened. Manga, romance novels, anime, medieval history, role-playing games, writing poetry and fan fiction, dogs, drawing cartoons, high-stakes drama in their personal lives. Second, I figured out how to incorporate some movement into those interests. Together, we created a medieval-style guild, complete with model-making, pool noodle jousting, and even a homemade medieval-period feast. We ate with our hands while in costume! We did archery in the gym wearing chain mail. We made a blog and wrote book reviews and had writing contests. We sketched from art books.

While we were having so much fun, the club kept getting bigger and bigger. Next thing I knew, the jocks were coming into the library to take part in our programs alongside the drama kids, the preps, the goths, and all the other fascinating subgroups you find in a high school. Football players were jousting with math geeks. Preppy kids were coming in to check out our medieval paper models. Circulation went up, up, up. And not just among students, but also staff. One teacher popped her head into the packed library at lunch hour and said, "I don't know how you did it, but you made the library the *cool* place to hang out." I watched what I affectionately thought of as *my kids* blossom and make new friends and grow more confident. We sort of forgot about some of the original tasks of being Guild members (like shelving books . . . *boring!*) and just started inventing more and more fun things to do. They would make me lists of books, movies, and magazines to buy. They were (without knowing it) my Teen Advisory Group.

Unfortunately, my contract ended, and I had to move on, and we lost touch. But one day, about five years later, I ran into one of my former students, whom I'll call Terry. Terry was fairly high-functioning, but he talked slowly, had a hard time making eye contact, and was extremely shy, until you got him talking about something he was interested in, like computers, and then he was the loudest, most animated kid in the room with a giant smile and no "off" switch. When I first met him, he seemed very negative and depressed. He was one of my kids who was at the library first thing in the morning, every break and noon hour, and also after school until we closed. But once he joined the Library Guild his social skills improved and so did his attitude. And here he was all grown up and working in a food truck when I stopped to get some supper for my family.

Terry waited on me quietly and never made any indication that he recognized me. When I went back up to the counter to get ketchup I said, "Terry, do you remember a crazy librarian that used to be at your high school?" And he looked up at me, not quite making eye contact, and said, "I loved that librarian!" That's when I realized he had known it was me all along but had been too nervous to say anything. He broke out into a huge smile and told me all about how he had traveled to Europe (Europe! This was a kid who hardly left the library for four years!) and was building computers when he wasn't working. My heart—it soared! He was thriving!

All this is to say that if you build it and make it enticing and suited to their needs, they will come. And it will be (mostly) glorious. I promise.

PROGRAM MODEL Nerf Battle

This is a high-energy, easily adaptable program that appeals to teens, but it also works well with families, millennials, and is a great stress-reliever for staff. Gather some Nerf guns, create obstacle courses, hold a target practice, or stage some team-building strategy games. Try to resist pulling the trigger of a Nerf gun—I dare you!

FIGURE 5.1
Nerf Battle poster

Advance Planning

STEP 1. Figure out what time of day and what day of the week you want to run the program. Do you want to coordinate it with an existing teen program? After school, evenings, and weekends are best for academic and public libraries. If you are doing this in a high school library, you could hold it at lunch hour.

STEP 2. Once you've got a date nailed down, book the room or find a suitable outdoor space. The program will last at least one hour. Decide how many people you have room for. Also, you will need to have enough Nerf guns for everyone, or else ask people to bring their own. This will affect whether or not you want this to be a drop-in program or have pre-registration.

STEP 3. Decide what types of games you will have. You can create target practice, obstacle courses, play Capture the Flag (if you have the space), or all three. Design the games and decide what materials you'll need. We used paper targets, hula hoops, chairs, yoga mats and blocks, and more. See the "Materials Required" section and the accompanying photos for more ideas. Detailed descriptions of some games are listed under the "Day of the Event" section.

STEP 4. Borrow, make, or buy all the "Materials Required" for the program. Here's where you can get really creative with props.

STEP 5. Advertise. Make a Facebook event. Make a little promo video to share on YouTube and other platforms. Put it in your paper program calendar (if you have one) and on the website. Tweet about it. Do a call-in to the local radio station (lots of teens still listen to the radio in their vehicles or hear the PA system at the mall/gym, etc., at least in my town). Make an awesome-looking poster and be sure to share it with your local high schools, gyms, and sports clubs.

STEP 6. Every parent/guardian and participant over age eighteen (check your local laws) needs to sign a liability waiver in case the participants get hurt. Make these waivers ahead of time. Everyone also needs to sign a photo release waiver (or refusal) for photos/video, if you are taking some to share on social media.

STEP 7. Figure out if you will need volunteers to help with the event and recruit them. Our first Nerf Battle had fifteen participants and we could have really used an extra set of hands helping out. It is better to have too many staff/volunteers than not enough.

Variations

❱ *Archery Classes.* When I ran the Hampton High School Library, we set up targets in the gym and had someone come in and teach us how to use real bows and arrows to shoot targets. It was awesome. If you have the room and budget for it, this is a very popular program for teens.

❱ *Sports Demos.* Have a local sports hero come in and do demos for young adults and then give everyone a chance to try. We had a local Frisbee Guinness World Record Holder (who also happened to be an author) come in and teach us Frisbee tricks.[2] A local skateboard pro, motocross legend, mountain biker, climber, or snowboarder would also draw a crowd.

❱ *Capture the Flag.* Not into weapons? Play Capture the Flag with regular old "freeze tag" for those who get "out," or the "tagged" person can go into "jail" or be forced to play for the other team. There are lots of variations you can look up on the Internet. You can also play in the dark (outside at night or in a dark room) using flashlights or laser pointers.

❱ *If you want to adapt this program for a younger audience* (ages 3–7), you can use beanbags or balloons to throw at the targets and just have the kids crawl through the obstacle course and come out the other side. There are lots of opportunities for physical literacy skill-building here.

❱ *Staff Shootout.* Is this a particularly stressful time of year (tax season, anyone?), or are there too many days of meetings or trainings? Bust out the Nerf guns and some targets and have everyone fire a few rounds. It'll let a little steam out of the valves. I'll let you decide whether it's safe to fire them at each other—you know your staff (and HR policies) better than I do.

FIGURE 5.2 Target game

Materials Required

❏ Nerf blasters (we bought the Nerf Rival brand, which is designed for an older audience and uses foam rounds instead of foam darts).[3] The quantity will depend on if you are providing them for everyone or just having a few extras on hand. Because our budget was limited, we bought two and asked people to bring their own, if they had them.

❏ Safety glasses (we got these at the dollar store).

❏ Liability waiver/photo release/evaluations (if using).

❏ Vests or armbands, or something to designate which team the player is on.

❏ Flags (for Capture the Flag).

❏ Cold refreshments (the players get thirsty running around, so we have Freezies available).

❏ Chairs, hula hoops, bells, rope, cardboard, yoga mats, paper cups, blocks, beanbags, balls, and anything else you could think of to use for an obstacle course or targets.

❏ Paper or plastic bulls-eye to hang on the wall if you have the kind of foam darts with the suction cups on the end.

Budget Details

$100–500+

This program could get pricey, depending on whether you are supplying the Nerf guns and how many you need. Nerf blasters run anywhere from $10 to $80+ each. Refill packs of darts can be found for $6 to $20 or more. We just

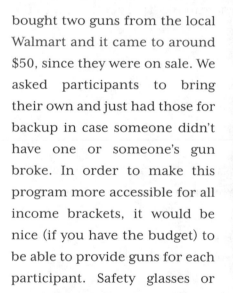

FIGURE 5.3 Nerf group

bought two guns from the local Walmart and it came to around $50, since they were on sale. We asked participants to bring their own and just had those for backup in case someone didn't have one or someone's gun broke. In order to make this program more accessible for all income brackets, it would be nice (if you have the budget) to be able to provide guns for each participant. Safety glasses or

FIGURE 5.4 Hiding spots

goggles and flags or vests can be found at the dollar store. We close registration after fifteen participants sign up due to space restrictions, so for us this meant an expense of less than $50 for the accessories. A box of Freezies shouldn't cost more than $10, and you could always ask participants to bring a water bottle from home to keep costs down. You can use existing items from around the library to make the targets and obstacle course. I know how creative and resourceful you are.

You may want to look into grants that provide sporting equipment to non-profit community organizations, or check out secondhand shops or yard sales for older models of Nerf guns that are still in good shape to add to your collection. You could even put a shout-out to patrons on social media; many people might have some guns collecting dust in their basements and toy boxes.

Day of the Event

STEP 1. Set up the targets and obstacle courses. First map out how much space you have for the course and determine where the start and finish will be. It's a good idea to cordon off an area of the room (or have a separate room, if you have the space) for target practice, so while people are waiting their turn through the obstacle course, they can shoot targets. Take some cardboard and draw bulls-eye targets on small squares of cardboard; these can be hung on the wall or propped against a chair or shelf.

Here are some more ideas for targets; you can incorporate these into the obstacle course or have them separate:

1. Take some plastic or Styrofoam cups and poke holes in the bottom and thread yarn through the holes. Hang these from a propped-up hula hoop, dangling down through the middle, in varying lengths, for the teens to shoot at. You can draw numbers on the cup-targets for different points.

2. Hang Frisbees from a dowel put across two shelving units, or hung from the ceiling if it isn't too high. You can draw numbers on the Frisbees for points.

3. Set small plastic balls on upside-down paper cups, and participants can try to shoot the balls off of the cups without knocking the cups over.

4. Here's the simple obstacle course my staff designed for an indoor activity room: tie some rope between table legs to create a tricky floor crawl obstacle. Another crawl obstacle can be under chairs with a sticky yoga mat underneath, which makes it harder to slide. Cover a hula hoop in bells for people to crawl through without ringing the bells. Hula hoops can be placed on the floor for people to jump into too, or a hopscotch mat can be used instead. Remember that you can make the obstacle course as big and elaborate or as simple and accessible as you need for the age range and abilities of the participants or what your space allows.

FIGURE 5.5 Nerf girl

STEP 2. Designate a "viewing area" for parents or siblings to watch from if they aren't participating. Make sure it is out of the "shooting range" so no one gets a stray dart to the eye. If it's behind glass, that's even better.

STEP 3. Have a clipboard with the liability waivers ready at the door, with pens, for parents or participants over age eighteen.

STEP 4. Prepare refreshments (a cooler works to keep Freezies or Popsicles cold).

STEP 5. Welcome everyone and explain the rules and expectations (i.e., no shooting each other, no shooting above the shoulders, must wear safety glasses, etc.), which will vary depending on what types of games you are playing.

STEP 6. While participants/parents are signing waivers, let everyone practice shooting at the targets and have the chance to chat informally and meet up with friends or make new ones. They will have to help each other by resetting the targets that they did manage to hit. This is the beginning of the team-building that will grow stronger with later activities, culminating in the team strategy game of Capture the Flag.

STEP 7. To make sure everyone feels a bit more comfortable with each other, play some icebreaker games. A good one is to toss a beanbag back and forth to learn names and go around the circle saying what school you go to and one random fact about yourself. Spend about 10–15 minutes doing these games to get everyone feeling more social.

Another icebreaker is to toss the beanbag to a random teen (while you are standing in a circle) and say "Hi, my name is _____." The catcher then says, "Thanks _____, my name is _____" as he tosses it to a different participant in the circle. This action is then repeated through the whole group. Once you catch the beanbag, you hold your hands behind your back to ensure that you don't get the beanbag again. Once you move through the whole group, you ask the teens to remember the order and then complete the circuit again, going faster. You can do the circuit a third and fourth time, adding a second beanbag and two or three people into the circuit. This can be altered for time and difficulty, depending on the age group.

STEP 8. Have everyone run through the obstacle course at intervals, so there are no pileups. While people are waiting their turns, they can help reset the targets and do some target practice. Depending on how many teens you have and your time allowance for this portion, they may be able to go through the course a number of times or just once.

STEP 9. Go outside, or to a large open gym if one is available, to play Capture the Flag. Break the group into two equal-numbered teams. Assign half of the lawn, park, or gym to each team. They get five minutes to hide their "flag" (any item can be a flag), and where they hide it is the home base. Once flags are hidden, game play begins. If a participant is "shot" by someone on the opposite team, they have to do ten jumping jacks (or freeze, if you have people playing who are less able-bodied). The object of the game is to capture the opposite team's flag and bring it back to your home base to score a point. Each time a point is scored, the teams switch sides on the game area. You can play three rounds, or five, or for as long as you like. Players can also be given timed breaks to gather ammo without being shot at. You can find other versions of Capture the Flag online.

Tips

1. When playing Capture the Flag or other team-strategy games, sometimes the participants get really focused on collecting their spent darts and they forget about capturing the flag (or other end-goal). If everyone has the same type of gun with the same kind of dart, it is easy to have a refill station with a bucket of darts they can come back to. Have a volunteer assigned to collecting darts during or after the games.

2. It's a good idea to take a break halfway through the program so everyone can get a drink or have a Freezie, especially if you are playing outside in hot weather.

3. Make sure your obstacle course or games are accessible, or at least adaptable, for people in a wheelchair or who are otherwise differently abled. You may need to brainstorm ideas for those with vision difficulties, but you could have bigger targets or noise-activated ones. It helps to know your patrons ahead of time to prepare.

4. If you are playing outside of the library, be careful not to play near a parking lot or the street. I mean, not even in the vicinity. Because of potential injury, yes, but also because patrons and community members will complain about the foam darts potentially hitting their cars (explaining that the darts are made out of foam doesn't seem to help).

5. Make sure everyone wears protective eyewear, even if they complain about it. In fact, make them wear it even if their parent is right there and says it is okay. The rules are the rules. Safety first. Also, uninvolved library patrons and other onlookers will complain about how you are endangering the lives of children if they see someone not wearing protective eyewear. They may even send you messages about it on Facebook. Or maybe my town is just particularly . . . vocal? Play it safe, on all accounts.

6. Try out your Nerf blasters before the program. I had my staff member Ebony shoot me in the butt with the round foam pellets to make sure they didn't hurt too much. One of our guns' magazines got jammed, and we panicked and jimmied it for almost twenty minutes before we figured out how to fix it. The instructions were of no help. But we solved it, because we are awesome librarians, like you. But be awesome even *before the program.* You don't want to start the games with malfunctioning equipment.

7. Always buy extra darts. They will get lost and broken.

Multiple Literacy Tie-In

While there aren't a lot of books available on the topic of Nerf guns, and it might be a tad controversial to make a "gun book" display in the young adult department, here are some fun ideas to expand this program:

❯ Believe it or not, there is an actual book called *The Ultimate Nerf Blaster Book* by Nathaniel Manuras. It even comes with six foam darts. Wait, there's more! Maybe four books are not enough for a whole display, but you could pad the table with some other sports-related items:

◦ *Nerf*, by Sara Green (aimed at a younger audience)
◦ *Build Your Own Autonomous NERF Blaster: Programming Mayhem with Processing and Arduino*, by Bryce Bigger (which could be a STEM program)
◦ *Nerf War: Over 25 Best Nerf Blasters Field Tested for Distance and Accuracy! Plus, Nerf Gun Safety, Setting Up Nerf Wars, Nerf Mods, and Buying Nerf Blasters for Cheap*, by Eric Michael (yes, that's the whole title)

❯ Alternative collection idea: if you amass a large collection of Nerf guns, consider cataloging them and teens could check them out at the desk (with safety glasses) and fire them at targets set up in a room or outdoor space during a designated weekly or monthly time slot. Teens can come and go as they please; you just have to set up and tear down the targets and make sure the teens sign a liability waiver.

PROGRAM MODEL **Earth Walk**

In celebration of Earth Day (April 22), arm teens with gloves and garbage bags and head out to clean up the library's grounds, the schoolyard, or the neighborhood. Finish up with a walk in the park or hold a picnic outside. The more teens pay attention to the world around them (instead of just living on their smartphones), the more they will care about it. We learn to protect and keep healthy the things we care about. Many teens are already socially and environmentally aware, and this program will be great to connect them with a larger community of people.

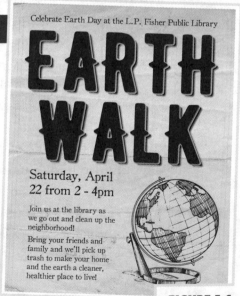

FIGURE 5.6
Earth Walk poster

Advance Planning

STEP 1. Figure out what time of day and what day of the week you want to run the program. Consider a rain date for bad weather, and keep in mind that it's hard to see garbage at dusk. The program probably won't last more than an hour, depending on how much ground you plan to cover. If you are doing this in a high school library, you could hold the program at lunch hour. Do you want to coordinate it with an existing teen program? For example, you could tag it on to a teen book club and have that month's book be an environmental dystopia.

STEP 2. Decide if it will be a drop-in program or require pre-registration. You want to make sure you'll have enough gloves for everyone, unless you ask people to bring their own.

STEP 3. Borrow, make, or buy all the "Materials Required" (see below) for the program. To make the garbage stakes, take an old broom handle and hot-glue a nail to the end (pointy end down) to stab garbage with.

STEP 4. Advertise. Make a Facebook event. Make a little promo video to share on YouTube and other platforms. Put the event in your paper program calendar (if you have one) and on the website. Tweet about it. Make an awesome-looking poster and be sure to share it with your local high schools, gyms, and sports clubs.

STEP 5. Print off the photo release forms if you are planning on taking pictures/video.

Variations

❭ *Tree or flower planting.* Use this opportunity to beautify the library's flower beds or green space (if you have one). If you are in an urban center that doesn't even have planter boxes, consider sending every participant of the Earth Walk home with a seedling in a pot for their window sill. They get bonus points if they plant the seed themselves.

❭ *Seed Library.* If you already have a seed library, get teens involved by having them sort and bag seeds, or design graphics for the bags/envelopes or posters in order to help spread the word about the Earth Walk.

Materials Required

❑ Garbage bags
❑ Thick utility gloves (you don't want to use latex/rubber gloves in case the teens pick up something sharp)
❑ Garbage stakes
❑ Trash grabbers

FIGURE 5.7 Collecting garbage on an Earth Walk

❏ Refreshments (if using)
❏ Photo release forms (if using)

Budget Details

$30–50+

The cost will all depend on how many participants you have. You should be able to find heavy utility gloves at the dollar store. A box of garbage bags will be about $20. The garbage stakes are optional, but if you have the supplies on hand already they are super useful. Trash pickers (those grabbers with the claws on them) are great if you can afford them. They will cost about $15 each. Encourage participants to bring along refillable water bottles to stay hydrated (and save money).

Day of the Event

STEP 1. Gather all your materials and have a clipboard for the photo releases (if using).

STEP 2. Once everyone has arrived, outline where you will be walking and set a time and location to meet up. You may want to have people work in teams of two or three. If your municipality recycles, one person could have a bag for the recyclables, the other could have a bag for garbage, and the third can wield the stake (unless you have enough stakes for everyone).

STEP 3. Go over the rules about what should and shouldn't be touched, and what to do if someone finds something dangerous (like a needle or broken glass).

STEP 4. Head out to start cleaning up the defined area. You and any other staff can float between groups, keeping track of everyone and making sure there are no problems.

STEP 5. Meet up at the determined location and collect all the garbage bags. This is a good chance for everyone to have a drink and a little snack if you've provided them (make sure they wash their hands or at least take off their gloves—ick!). If you have time and it's feasible, you could go for a little walk to admire the area you just cleaned up, or you could just enjoy a nice little picnic in the sunshine. Make sure you don't leave any garbage behind.

Tips

1.   Don't forget that many teens are already very interested in social justice and environmental consciousness. Recruit a few like-minded teens to spread the word about the event and invite their friends who otherwise might not be interested.

2.   Get a teen or two to help you create the Facebook event and poster; they will probably know what appeals to their own audience better than you. And they will want to share something they helped design. Win-win.

3.   Have zero tolerance for roughhousing with the garbage stakes. The minute a stake gets swiped (even jokingly) at someone else, that stake is confiscated. It's just not worth the risk.

Multiple Literacy Tie-In

❩ Make a great display of books about living a low-impact lifestyle to encourage teens to continue the conversation and keep engaged when they go home. Here are some ideas to get you started:

∘   *Coming of Age at the End of Nature: A Generation Faces Living on a Changed Planet,* ed. by Julie Dunlap and Susan A. Cohen

- *Eating Green: Environmentally Friendly Food,* by Films Media Group
- *The Edible Front Lawn,* by Ivette Soler
- *The Environmental Movement: From Its Roots to the Challenges of a New Century,* by Laurence Pringle
- *Eyes Wide Open: Going Behind the Environmental Headlines,* by Paul Fleischman
- *Food Not Lawns,* by H. C. Flores
- *Garbology: Our Dirty Love Affair with Trash,* by Edward Humes
- *Generation Green: The Ultimate Teen Guide to Living an Eco-Friendly Life,* by Linda Sivertsen
- *No Impact Man* (book/DVD), by Colin Beavan
- *Plastic-Free: How I Kicked the Plastic Habit and How You Can Too,* by Beth Terry

PROGRAM MODEL Quidditch

Bring the magical world of Harry Potter into your library with more than just books. Do it by playing every wizard's and witch's favorite sport—Quidditch!

Advance Planning

STEP 1. Figure out what time of day and what day of the week you want to run the program. If you are playing outdoors, you need to consider the available daylight hours. The event will also be weather-dependent. You may want to pick a rain date. If you are lucky enough to have a facility with a gymnasium, this won't be an issue.

FIGURE 5.8
Quidditch poster

STEP 2. Once you've got a date nailed down, book the gym or find a suitable outdoor space. We are fortunate to live in a town with multiple outdoor green spaces near our library. The program will last at least one hour. You might want to have pre-registration, since you will need at least fourteen players (seven on each team), or you run the risk of not having enough players and sending people home disappointed.

STEP 3. Learn how to play Quidditch and make sure you are firm on the rules, lest you be challenged (it will happen). Check out this handy infographic

FIGURE 5.9 Quidditch players

(figure 5.12) you can print or photo-copy and hand out to players.[4]

STEP 4. Borrow, make, or buy all of the "Materials Required" for the program, including your costumes.

STEP 5. Advertise. Make a Face-book event. Make a little promo video to share on YouTube, being sure to wear your robes. Put a promo in your paper program calendar (if you have one) and on the website. Tweet about it. Do a call-in to the local radio sta-tion (lots of teens still listen to the radio in their vehicles or hear the PA system at the mall/gym, etc., at least in my town). Make an awesome-looking poster and be sure to share it

FIGURE 5.10 Jump

with your local high schools, bookstores, and coffee shops.

STEP 6. Every parent/guardian and participant over age eighteen (check your local laws; it might be age sixteen in some areas) needs to sign a liability waiver in case the participants get hurt. Make these waivers ahead of time.

FIGURE 5.11 Broom

Everyone also needs to sign a photo release waiver (or refusal) for photos/video, if you are taking some to share on social media.

Variations

❭ *Quidditch for Kids.* You can modify this program for a younger demographic by using hand-tagging instead of bludgers and hiding the snitch instead of having a real-life player running around. Make sure everyone brings a broom and a costume.

❭ *Quidditch for Adults.* You can modify this program to make it more appealing to adults by serving (Butter)beer instead of Freezies or Popsicles. Increase the difficulty by having a very fast runner play the snitch and using small foam balls for bludgers.

❭ *Gobstones or Wizarding Chess.* For a less robust activity (or for those without a Quidditch pitch available), try offering other Potter-themed games to be played in costume, such as Gobstones (marbles) or chess. Potter-themed refreshments can also be included, like pumpkin juice or chocolate frogs.

❭ *Broom-Making Workshop.* In anticipation of your upcoming Quidditch program, why not host a broom-making workshop so everyone will have a broom to play with? There are plenty of tutorials online you can follow, some more elaborate than others (i.e., ones requiring a wood shop).

RULES FOR QUIDDITCH

You are going to require:

- ☐ **A minimum of 14 players**
- ☐ **a soccer or volleyball** (quaffle)
- ☐ **4 smaller foam balls** or shortened pool noodles (bludgers),
- ☐ **6 hula hoops** (goals) that can be strung up off the ground, either hanging from a tree or football goal, or else stuck into the ground on a stick (see pictures).
- ☐ **People can either bring their own brooms or the library can provide them.** You can also play without.

On each team there are **7 players** including **1 keeper** (goalie) who guards the goal posts (3 hula hoops); **3 chasers** (goal scoring members) who try and get the ball through the goal posts, **2 beaters** (troublemakers) who run around and disrupt game play by tagging members of the opposite team with the smaller balls or pool noodles, and **1 seeker** who only looks for the **golden snitch.**

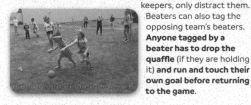

Neutral Players
There needs to be a **referee** (i.e.: not a parent). There needs to be one person who will be the **snitch**. If you don't have enough people, you can hide the snitch somewhere on the pitch instead.

Team members should wear all the same color shirts, or vests, or headbands. The snitch should be dressed in yellow, or else have a yellow flag hanging from their waistband.

There Are Three Games Being Played Simultaneously.

1. The first part of the game involves the chasers trying to score goals on the opposite team's keeper with the quaffle. They throw or kick the quaffle through the hoops and try to take the quaffle from each other. **Each goal is worth 10 points** and there is no limit on goals scored.

2. The second part of the game involves the beaters. The beaters on each team run around trying to tag out everyone on the opposing team with a bludger. They cannot tag the keepers, only distract them. Beaters can also tag the opposing team's beaters. **Anyone tagged by a beater has to drop the quaffle** (if they are holding it) **and run and touch their own goal before returning to the game.**

3. The final part of the game involves the seeker. Each seeker is looking for the golden snitch. You have two options for a golden snitch: you can hide a small yellow object somewhere in the playing zone (good option for younger players or if you don't have enough people), or you can dress a fast runner up in yellow (or put a yellow flag in their waistband) and have them be a mobile snitch that needs to be caught. Seekers chase the golden snitch but can only catch it when it is within the parameters of the pitch. The golden snitch, if it is a runner, is more than welcome to appear and disappear during the course of the game. **A caught snitch is worth 30 points and once the snitch is caught the game is over.** However, just because you catch the snitch does not mean that your team wins the game. The team with the most points wins the game. Some teams might find it better to not catch the snitch right away if they need to catch up on points.

FIGURE 5.12 Quidditch infographic

Materials Required

- ❏ 6 hula hoops
- ❏ Whistle for the referee
- ❏ Yellow flag or headband for the snitch

❏ Refreshments (popsicles, Freezies, water, or pumpkin juice)

❏ Brooms (provided, or they can bring their own)

❏ Costumes (if using)

❏ 14 headbands (7 in each color)

❏ Black robe for the referee

❏ Volleyball or soccer ball

❏ 4 smaller (soft!) balls or pool noodles cut in half

❏ Stakes or string to attach/suspend goal hoops

❏ Liability waivers

❏ Photo/video release forms

❏ Feedback forms (if using)

❏ Beanbag (for icebreaker)

Budget Details

$50–200+

This event can be very economical if you already have a number of the needed props, like balls, hula hoops, headbands/vests, etc. You may only need to buy refreshments. And maybe a whistle (because a shared whistle is *ewww*). Everyone can bring a broom from home.

Day-of-Event

STEP 1. Set up all the hoops and mark off the pitch ahead of time and prepare the cooler with refreshments.

STEP 2. All participants meet at the library and sign a photo release and a liability waver (or their parents do this).

STEP 3. Play a little icebreaker game, like standing in a circle passing a bean-bag and saying, "My name is ___" and tossing the beanbag to someone else. They respond with "Thanks ___. My name is ___." Then you can speed up and go around the circle a few times until everyone knows everyone else's name.

STEP 4. Discuss how the game is played. Feel free to use the handy infographic given above. You should also go over the rules, your expectations for behavior, and the consequences for not following the rules.

STEP 5. Walk to the pitch (unless you are playing indoors).

STEP 6. Divide up the teams, and give them colored sashes/headbands/vests and brooms. Let them decide which position they are going to play and work out a strategy with their teammates.

STEP 7. Players line up in front of their goals and props are placed in the middle of the pitch. The referee blows the whistle and everyone runs to grab the appropriate balls for their position.

STEP 8. Play as many rounds as you have time for, encouraging players to switch positions so everyone gets a chance to try out each role. Take water breaks in between.

STEP 9. Everyone helps clean up the pitch and walks back to the library.

STEP 10. At the library, give everyone a Freezie, Popsicle, or other treat, and this is your chance to get feedback on what worked and what didn't.

Tips

1. You can use fewer hula hoops. We only had four, so rather than buying more, our teams had two goals each.

2. In order to encourage less roughhousing and make each game go slower, require everyone to stay on their brooms the whole game.

3. Instead of throwing balls as bludgers, the player has to tag with their hands or (gently) with a pool noodle.

4. If your snitch is really fast, give them some sort of handicap (like they have to stay within bounds, or run backwards) so that seekers don't get too frustrated.

5. Be mindful of group age dynamics. There is (usually) a huge weight/height/strength difference between a thirteen-year-old and an eighteen-year-old. Make sure when you are selecting the teams that you keep this in mind.

Multiple Literacy Tie-In

Here are some fun ideas to keep the magic going after the game is over:

❭ A display of all the Harry Potter books in all the available formats, including the films. If you want to get really ambitious, you can even add some J. K. Rowling biographies and her other non-Potter books. Don't forget to include *Quidditch through the Ages* (2017).[5]

❭ Have a program for writing and reading Potter Fan Fiction and create a display of the best quotes from each story.

❭ Create a Quidditch pitch diorama.

❭ If you have a gaming console at your library, host a Quidditch World Cup tournament.[6]

PROGRAM MODEL Yoga Break

This program consists of a quick series of yoga poses or postures that can be done in the classroom, library, or study hall for students who just need a chance to chill out and relieve tension from being hunched over their computers, textbooks, or phones. This is a great program to be done during exam week; make it a recurring program and the teens will look forward to it. The program is easily modified for sitting or standing (and it works great for staff, too). No mats or props are needed—it's also zero cost!

FIGURE 5.13
Yoga Break Poster

Advance Planning

STEP 1. Find a staff member with some yoga experience (bonus points if they're a certified instructor) to teach this easy series of stretches that almost anyone can do. Have them (or you, if you're game) learn the poses well enough so they feel comfortable leading a group through them (see the infographic in figure 5.16 for the series). You can always practice on some staff during a meeting or in the break room as a test run.

STEP 2. Decide the best time to deliver the program. If you work as a high school librarian, you should coordinate with teachers to see when the students can come to the library, or when you can visit their classroom. If you work in a college or university library, book a time in the evening, to give students a break from studying for exams or writing papers. If you work in a public library, consider evenings, after school, or weekends.

STEP 3. You can book a room, if you are using one, but this program is designed to be taught right in the classroom or reading room/study area and is desk-friendly. No open space for mats is needed.

STEP 4. Advertise the program. Design an eye-catching poster. Create bookmarks to hand out at the circulation desk so students will see the reminder while they work. Make a Facebook event to share. If you work in a school library, have the event added to the newsletter, morning announcements, or other

FIGURE 5.14 Yoga break (with optional mats)

methods that teachers use to get event information out to students.

STEP 5. There are no real props needed for this program, unless you'd like to buy a chime or singing bell to use at the beginning and end of class, or during a little meditation, if you decide to add a few moments of silence.

STEP 6. You might want to print off some copies of the infographic to hand out at the end of class, so students will have something to take home and practice on their own. Print liability waivers.

FIGURE 5.15 Teen meditation

Variations

❭ *Yoga Break (for adults).* This program can easily be adapted for any work environment for adults, including seniors. I regularly use it in staff meetings and at training events. It could even work in prison libraries, law libraries, or other special collections, provided you have enough space to accommodate a few people. Use the routine in the infographic, or use my video, which can be found at https://www.youtube.com/watch?v=484_cJPBmEk. Another good resource is Sandy Blaine's *Yoga for Computer Users: Healthy Necks, Shoulders, Wrists, and Hands in the Postmodern Age.*

❱ **Passive Yoga Program.** Here's an option if you don't have room or time to teach: print off copies of the infographic and hand it out to patrons or staff.[7] This can be very useful for students, at professional development days, or for inmates in a prison library to have in their cells or practice at their desks.

❱ **Yoga Stories or Yoga Art Break.** If you have a bit more time and resources, expand the program to include an interesting story from around the world, some mark-making, or both. See the sidebar with Activity All-Star Sydney Solis for some more ideas.

Materials Required

- ❏ Singing bell or other chime (if using)
- ❏ Liability waivers
- ❏ Evaluation forms (if using)

Budget Details

$0-$30

This is pretty much a free program, unless you want to buy a bell to help center everyone (but you can just get a free app to use on your phone).

Day of the Event

STEP 1. Have everyone sign liability waivers before class.

STEP 2. Set the tone by having everyone sit at the edge of their chairs, with their feet flat on the floor, and focus on their breathing. This also gives a chance for latecomers to join without totally interrupting the flow of the class. Have them put a hand on their tummy and breathe in and out.[8] Do this for a few moments and let everyone settle into their breath, and then:

STEP 3. Go through the poses one by one. Repeat them multiple times on each side, as recommended in the infographic. Most poses can be done sitting or standing.

STEP 4. Finish the class by having everyone sit back on the edge of their chairs, hand on their belly button area (solar plexus), and focus on dropping their breath down into the lower lobes of their lungs. They may close their

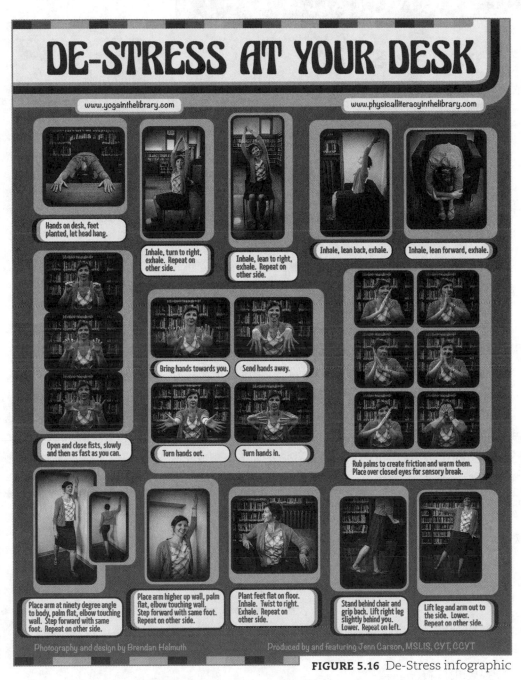

FIGURE 5.16 De-Stress infographic

eyes if they wish. Breathe together in silence for a few moments and then ring the bell (or app on your phone) to have everyone come out of it.

STEP 5. Send them off refreshed and renewed with a copy of the infographic to encourage home-practice and self-care. Evaluations would also be good to hand out.

Sydney Solis

Name: Sydney Solis, Yoga Teacher and Author

Location: Worldwide

Contact: info@StorytimeYoga.com

Claim to Fame: Founder of Storytime Yoga for kids, and Mythic Yoga, which combines myth and yoga for teens and adults.

All-Star Program: Storytime Yoga

Featured in libraries and conferences across the United States, Storytime Yoga emphasizes storytelling's oral tradition, using multicultural folklore, fairytales, and mythology for a unique, all-in-one, cross-curriculum combination of literacy, character education, psychosocial skills, and mental and physical health.

Storytime Yoga develops listening and concentration by reciting a complete story for kids to create original imagery internally in their heads, instead of externally consuming it from a book. The kids learn narrative structure by acting the story out with yoga postures for a complete, embodied storytelling yoga experience.

The Six Storytime Yoga Kids Yoga Story Kits (Mythic Yoga Studio, 2011, Boulder, Colorado) are innovative in using world folklore and traditional Japanese Kamishibai and East Indian scrolls as visual aids, maintaining direct teller and listener contact. Storytime Yoga music has been used as a puppet show in the Los Angeles County Library and elsewhere.

Many psychotherapists have trained in Storytime Yoga in order to help kids develop empathy, inner resourcefulness, and self-reflection via stories for mental health and attention-deficit disorder management.

Here are some tips for a Storytime Yoga program in your library: create a ritual and take students on a yoga journey by suspending time and space to experience yoga within their own bodies and psyches. Do this by creating a beginning, middle, and end to the class.

Beginnings: Ring a bell. Introduce a class with a puppet, special stone, or box. Use chants, songs, imagery, and poetry for warm-ups, breathing, and centering. Use the Storytime Yoga Sun Salutation chant or hand/body meditations. Have students create their own warm-ups from yoga or other movements using three poses.

Middle: Tell completely and orally a short folk tale, fairytale, or myth, depending on the age of the audience. Use facial expressions, simple movements, and your body to tell the story and elicit lots of participation. Alternately, you can point to the Kamishibai, scrolls, or a felt board for a visual aid.

Then have students help you retell the story with yoga. Ask the students questions about what the story was about—who, what's in the landscape, animals, and so on—in order to teach narrative, oral skills, and critical thinking. Then act out that portion of the story with yoga poses. Then ask, "What happens next?" to move the story along and take another pose until asking, "How does the story end?"

Ending: End with creative relaxation using imagery, modified meditation, and *yoga nidra*; this is sleep yoga that Storytime Yoga calls Sleepytime Yoga or Story Siesta, and it can be found in *The Treasure in Your Heart: Yoga and Stories for Peaceful Children*. Ring the bell to bring the students out of their relaxed state. Ask them how they feel in order to encourage expression. See if they can retell the basics of the story's beginning, middle, and end. Close the class with a bell. Try an entire class with relaxation and storytelling only!

Follow-Up: After class, show the students the books you got the story from, and show them where to find more like it in the library. Encourage yoga practice and telling the story at home or school. For an extended time period, have students draw their favorite part of the story from the pictures they formed in their heads. Have them point to their picture and tell that part of the story. Have students write their own story and even make simple books. Preliterate kids can dictate the story to an adult who will write the story down.

Tips

1. Don't rush through the poses, and don't hesitate to run through the whole series multiple times, depending on how much time you have allotted. It takes a while to build up muscle memory, but once they do, it will be more automatic and they will think of doing these stretches when their necks, shoulders, and hands get tight from hunching over their textbooks, phones, or computers.

2. If you have the staff and time available, consider offering this program once a week, or even every day (especially during exam week or finals). The students will love it.

3. If you work in a school or academic library, consider traveling to where the students are. This gives you a great opportunity to plug the library and become a familiar face to those who don't frequent the library regularly. When I used to work at the College of Craft and Design in Fredericton, New Brunswick, I delivered weekly "Yoga Studio Breaks." Since it was a fine arts college, I would go to each of the studios (pottery, metalsmithing, drawing, graphic design, photography, etc.) and modify the poses based on their particular needs (i.e., lots of wrist and neck exercises for those on a computer all day). Be the traveling yogi-librarian.

4. Check out my how-to yoga videos for librarians or other digital resources at www.yogainthelibrary.com; these will give you some ideas about how to structure a Yoga Break class.[9]

Multiple Literacy Tie-In

〉 There are a number of yoga books geared towards teens and young adults, so make a display or bring them with you to the classroom to show what resources are available. For a comprehensive list, visit www.yogainthelibrary .com/yoga-for-children--teens.html

〉 Consider investing in some yoga card decks for your library. These are great to use during programs, to have as an alternative format collection, or to just put out in your space. Ideally you'd have some in your teen lounge, some in the children's department, and maybe some in your lobby or near your study rooms. They are also great to have in the staff room. Here's some good ones:

- *ABCs of Yoga for Kids: 56 Learning Cards*, by Theresa Anne Power
- *Be Mindful Card Deck for Teens*, by Gina M. Biegel
- *The Kids' Yoga Deck: 50 Poses and Games*, by Annie Buckley
- *The Mark Stephens Yoga Sequencing Deck*, by Mark Stephens
- *Mindful Games Activity Cards: 55 Fun Ways to Share Mindfulness with Kids and Teens*, by Susan Kaiser Greenland and Annaka Harris
- *The Prenatal Yoga Deck: 50 Poses and Meditations*, by Olivia Miller and Nicole Kaufman
- *Strong Body & Mind Yoga Cards*, by Kathy Beliveau (these cards feature Indigenous imagery)
- *The Yoga Deck: 50 Poses & Meditations for Body, Mind, & Spirit*, by Olivia Miller

- *Yoga Dice: 7 Wooden Dice, Thousands of Possible Combinations!* by Chronicle Books
- *Yoga Planet,* by Leah Kalish and Tara Guber
- *Yoga Pretzels,* by Leah Kalish and Tara Guber

❱ Tell students (and teachers) about free online resources or use them during yoga breaks. The website at www.GoNoodle.com has some great short videos (5–10 minutes) of exercises you can do to get your brain and body engaged. They have videos geared to preschoolers, elementary-age students, middle school students, and teens. Here's some DVDs for teens:

- *Shanti Generation: Partner Yoga for Teens* (2012)
- *Shanti Generation: Yoga Skills for Youth Peacemakers* (2011)
- *Teenyogi: Recharge the Power Within You* (2010)

❱ There is a great series of wellness workbooks by New Harbinger for teens that would make a great display alongside the program. Some of the titles include:

- *Communication Skills for Teens: How to Listen, Express, and Connect for Success,* by Michelle Skeen et al.
- *The Grit Guide for Teens: A Workbook to Help You Build Perseverance, Self-Control, and a Growth Mindset,* by Caren Baruch-Feldman and Thomas R. Hoerr
- *Mindfulness for Teen Anxiety: A Workbook for Overcoming Anxiety at Home, at School, and Everywhere,* by Christopher Willard
- *Mindfulness for Teens with ADHD: A Skill-Building Workbook to Help You Focus and Succeed,* by Else Debra Burdick and Lara Honos-Webb
- *Overcoming Procrastination for Teens: A CBT Guide for College-Bound Students,* by William J. Knaus
- *The Perfectionism Workbook for Teens: Activities to Help You Reduce Anxiety and Get Things Done,* by Ann Marie Dobosz
- *The PTSD Workbook for Teens: Simple, Effective Skills for Healing Trauma,* by Libbi Palmer
- *A Still Quiet Place for Teens: A Mindfulness Workbook to Ease Stress and Difficult Emotions,* by Amy Saltzman
- *The Stress Reduction Workbook for Teens: Mindfulness Skills to Help You Deal with Stress,* by Gina M. Biegel
- *The Worry Workbook for Teens: Effective CBT Strategies to Break the Cycle of Chronic Worry and Anxiety,* by Jamie A. Micco

Notes

1. You can still find our now-obsolete blog at http://hhslibraryguild.blogspot.ca/.
2. To learn more about this program, visit www.programminglibrarian.org/blog/sports-heroes-who-read.
3. Visit https://www.hasbro.com/en-ca/brands/nerfrival to learn more about the Rival Nerf blasters.
4. This can be downloaded from www.jenncarson.com/resources.html.
5. J. K. Rowling and Tomislav Tomic, *Quidditch through the Ages* (London: Bloomsbury, 2017).
6. EA Games/Electronic Arts, *Harry Potter Quidditch World Cup* (Redwood City, CA: EA Games/Electronic Arts, 2005).
7. This can be downloaded from www.jenncarson.com/resources.html.
8. There is a video of how to lead this breathing technique and many of these poses available at https://www.youtube.com/watch?v=484_cJPBmEk.
9. YouTube, "Jenn Carson," https://www.youtube.com/channel/UCbB1nAVe8AFEFDjMXi3RJlA/videos?sort=dd&view=0&shelf_id=0.

Remembering How to Play

Getting Adults Moving

For things to reveal themselves to us, we need to be ready to abandon our views about them.

—*Thich Nhat Hanh*

If you are reading this you are more than likely an adult, or at least adult-ish. So I probably don't need to tell you, after 20, 30, or 40 or more years of habit and conditioning, just how hard it is to change. How we become accustomed to accepting less, from ourselves and from others. Lowering our expectations becomes not a gift we bestow on others, but more of a giving-up, a survival mechanism. How trying anything different feels overwhelming, impossible, or at the very least, just another thing we don't have the energy for.

You may find this hard to believe, given my current state of fitness, but I was once a smoker, and a half-a-pack-a-day smoker at that (even a chain-smoker under stress). I smoked for years. I know. Blech. But I loved smoking. I really, really did. I loved the ritual of it, sitting with my cup of tea in my rocking chair, unwinding. I loved the light-up and the inhaling and the sharp hit to the lungs. I loved watching the blue-grey cloud escape my lips and being able to control its speed and direction. In a world and a life that felt tilt-a-whirl unpredictable, this habit felt calming and meditative. Also, as an all-star "good girl," smoking felt vaguely revolutionary to me, like thumbing my nose at everyone who wanted to put me into a box, including myself. Don't worry, the cliché wasn't lost on me. Nor was the fact that nicotine is actually a stimulant, and was flooding my already jacked-up, anxiety-addled nervous system with even more adrenaline. So what made me kick my habit? Well, I started to feel sick. Like sick to my stomach after every smoke break, and then first thing in the morning, and then all morning long. It got to the point where I would almost retch putting a cigarette in my mouth or smelling the ashtray. I was not deterred by this, however. I wanted to keep smoking. I tried different brands, even rolling my own. Nothing helped. Smoking had always made my lungs feel like garbage and made my teeth yellow and my apartment reek, but I had somehow become accustomed to it. I tried to quit and kept failing. And this is where physical literacy came into play, long before I knew what to call it.

One afternoon, sitting in my rocking chair, struggling to resist the urge to smoke, I closed my eyes and tried to pay attention to my body. I took a deep breath and felt the cool air fill my nostrils. I held the breath, the same way I would normally hold the smoke in my lungs, and then I let out a nice long exhale. I felt just a tiny bit calmer. I still really wanted a cigarette. So I held my fingers up to my lips, miming the act, and took another deep breath, and this time I blew the air out of my open mouth between my fingers, the same way I would a stream of smoke. I'm sure I looked ridiculous. But my tight shoulders lowered just a little bit, my forehead creases relaxed. I didn't feel nauseous. I did it over and over until the urge to have a cigarette passed, and then I got up and made supper. From then on, whenever I would want a cigarette, I would notice how my body was feeling (usually extremely tense) and I would sit wherever I was, and take as many deep inhales as I needed until the shaky, panicky got-to-have-a-smoke-*now* feeling passed. And then I felt better. And I kept feeling better. In fact, my perpetual cough and stuffy nose cleared up, my stomach stopped feeling like it was eating itself, and I suddenly had more energy. I couldn't believe how I had gotten used to feeling so crummy without even noticing it. But by now I was practicing noticing what my body wanted and needed, and it turns out that all those times I thought I wanted to smoke, I really just wanted an excuse to take a time-out and breathe. It was a radical thought, but it was so simple and clear once I realized it, as the truth often is, and I never smoked again. I would test myself occasionally, taking a drag off a friend's cigarette, but my body would instantly reject the sensation, as long as I paid attention to it. It knew what it wanted, what I needed: clean, fresh air. Even now I feel my throat constrict around smoke, even at a campfire. I eventually went on to become a yoga and meditation teacher to help others

FIGURE 6.1 Adults at a Bike Clinic

understand this amazing power of the breath and how we all have the tools we need inside us to bring ourselves back to cohesion when circumstances, and conditioning, and faulty wiring, have had us suffering far too long without it.

This isn't an anti-tobacco diatribe, and I'm not trying to suggest that people with serious addictions can just breathe themselves into sobriety, but I am saying that human beings (even crusty set-in-our-ways adults) have the power to change long-ingrained habits and learn new skills, all by paying attention to our bodies and working *with* them, instead of against them. I'm living proof that it's possible. By offering these opportunities for growth to our patrons, we can improve physical literacy skills through-out the life course.

PROGRAM MODEL **Walk Club**

This is a fun, low-key walking program available to everyone that promotes inclusion and the building blocks of physical literacy.

Advance Planning

STEP 1. Figure out who you are trying to target with this program and what time of day you are going to offer it. Mornings will

The L.P. Fisher Public Library Presents

Walk Club

Tuesdays at 12:00 – Beginning April 4th

For all ages • Rain or shine • It's free!

Join us every Tuesday as we walk at an easy pace following a mapped route around the neighbourhood or walking trails for 30 minutes.

Call 325-4777 for more information.
www.facebook.com/L.P.Fisher.Library
L.P. Fisher Public Library, 679 Main St. Woodstock

FIGURE 6.2
Walk poster

appeal to seniors and young parents with strollers. By the afternoon all those babies and toddlers are napping, but you might get some seniors or shift-workers or others. Noon is a good time for day-workers who are looking to get some exercise on their lunch break, but make sure the walk is short enough that they have time to eat something and get back to the office. Evening walks will appeal to families, couples, and working professionals, but depending on where you live, it might be too dark, cold, or unsafe to walk at night. Weekends could work for families, but you'll want to have a special theme to draw their attention. Obviously, planning around the weather and the time of year is also a big concern, since where you live it might be too hot at midday, or too snowy in January.

STEP 2. Map out a route. Is this going to be a woodsy trail walk or a city stroll? How much time do you have, and what are the abilities of your participants? It is always best to err on the side of caution and leave some wiggle room at the end for stragglers or bathroom stops. At my library we usually do a 2.8-kilometer loop, which takes about thirty minutes at a moderate pace. Some of our seniors get a head start, so we all finish at the same time.

STEP 3. Decide if this is going to require pre-registration or if it is a drop-in program (ours is drop-in, but some variations might work better with a sign-up). Advertise. We use social media, posters, radio call-in, a web calendar, a paper calendar, and word of mouth. Share to groups that may be interested (parent groups, homeschool families, seniors groups, health groups, etc.).

Variations

❭ *Walk n' Wheels.* This is a program designed for people in wheelchairs, walkers, scooters, and other mobility devices. Meet for coffee or tea afterwards.

❭ *Baby Steps.* This is a program for caregivers with babies and toddlers in strollers or carriers/wraps.

❭ *Walk n' Stretch.* Add some yoga or stretching before or afterwards. This was popular at our library.

❭ *Heritage Walk.* Add a mini walking tour of local architecture/sights, and so on. This appeals to tourists as well as locals.

❭ *Nature Walk.* This is an outreach program in a local park or nature preserve with a focus on flora and fauna.

FIGURE 6.3 ChiWalking/Running Workshop

❱ *Stargazers Club.* Lead a nighttime walk while searching the solar system and beyond—just don't walk into anything!

❱ *Pokemon Walk Club.* Play Pokemon Go together while walking and strategizing.

❱ *Hiking Club.* This is a great outreach program for those who want longer treks into the wild. Add a book to it and make it a book-and-hike club—talk about the book while you hike!

❱ *Art Walk.* This is a walk-and-sketch program where you stop along the way to sketch points of interest.

❱ *Walking Meditation.* This involves walking with mindfulness. Engage in meditative walking around a park, lawn, large room, or labyrinth (you can even buy a labyrinth mat or make one yourself).[1] Have someone come from the local Shambhala or Zen center to teach you how.

❱ *Geocache Club.* Use GPS to search in teams for hidden containers. (Psst! We have one hidden in my library. Do you?)

❱ *Nordic Walk Club.* This is for those who enjoy walking more with poles. We tried to get one going in my branch, but there wasn't an instructor available or enough interest.

❭ *Walk n' Read.* This is a book club where they walk, instead of sit, while discussing the monthly book.

Materials Required

❏ Staff or volunteers leading the program need appropriate footwear and outerwear, and it's always a good idea to have an umbrella or two handy
❏ Sunglasses and/or a hat
❏ Optional water bottles (or you can remind people to fill up their own bottles at the drinking fountain)
❏ Printouts of the maps that people can take in case they get lost (but since you are staying together as a group, this shouldn't be a problem)
❏ A cell phone in case there is an emergency
❏ A flashlight or headlamp if you are walking at night
❏ Other items as needed, depending on the variation of choice (walking poles, sketch pads, etc.)

Budget Details

$0

This is a relatively no-cost program, other than printing off some maps and posters and perhaps buying a case of water bottles. If you want to get really fancy (or you have some grant money to burn), you could give participants branded BPA-free reusable water bottles with your library's logo.

Day of the Event

STEP 1. Meet at your determined location (library parking lot, lobby, historic site, etc.). It's a good idea to have at least two staff members or volunteers on the walk, one to lead and one to follow up in the rear to make sure no one gets left behind. Make sure everyone is aware of the route and how far they are going. I can't stress this enough. Give them a visual walk-through of the route. Lack of information breeds uncertainty, uncertainty breeds lack of confidence, and this makes you look unprofessional.

STEP 2. Walk. Make conversation. Check in to see how people are doing.

STEP 3. Gather at the end of the walk to celebrate your accomplishment and do a few stretches, if so desired.

Tips

1. Walk your planned route ahead of time in order to get an idea of any potential problems (busy intersections, uneven terrain that might affect strollers, wheelchairs, or people with limited mobility, etc.) and to get a rough estimate of how long it takes to walk it at an average pace. Remember that your pace might not be average for your demographic, and plan accordingly. I'll never forget one of my first Walk Clubs with two little old ladies who were so slow I ran laps back and forth from the rest of the group to check on them, and after thirty minutes they gave up and turned back for the library. *After they had only gone about two blocks.*

2. Don't leave anyone behind. Ever. If someone is sick, tired, winded, discouraged, or needs to find a bathroom, stay with them. Be mindful and be patient. The whole point of the Walk Club is to build community and be inclusive. Don't make the mistake of getting caught up in conversation and missing stragglers as a result. Avoid being concerned with your own fitness goals or "making good time."

3. Have a contingency plan if the weather is poor. How will you notify the group if the Walk Club is canceled? Do you have an indoor venue nearby you could use instead, like a shopping mall or track?

4. Partner with your local running group or other organizations (perhaps specific to your targeted demographic) to recruit volunteers or help spread the word.

Multiple Literacy Tie-In

Create meaningful displays for participants to browse (use multiple formats—audio, text, braille, DVDs, etc.):

❱ You can display local maps, and books about community parks, trails, or hikes. Here are some examples from my neck of the woods:

- ○ *Heritage Trails & Footpaths on Grand Manan Island, New Brunswick*, by Kevin O'Donnell
- ○ *A Hiking Guide to New Brunswick*, by Marianne Eiselt
  Hiking Trails of Nova Scotia, by Michael Haynes

❱ Travel books centered on walking excursions. Here are some ideas to get you started:

- *The Complete Walker IV*, by Colin Fletcher and Chip Rawlins
- *Fifty Places to Hike Before You Die*, by Chris Santella
- *The Lost Art of Walking: The History, Science, and Literature of Pedestrianism*, by Geoff Nicholson
- *A Walk across America*, by Peter Jenkins
- *A Walk in the Woods: Rediscovering America on the Appalachian Trail*, by Bill Bryson
- *Walking to Listen: 4,000 Miles across America, One Story at a Time*, by Andrew Forsthoefel

⟩ General fitness books; walking/running books; stretching/yoga books or DVDs. Here are some examples:

- *The Joy of Walking: More Than Just Exercise*, by Stephen Christopher Joyner
- *Walk It Off with George: Walk and Box (DVD)*, by George Foreman
- *Walking: A Complete Guide to the Complete Exercise*, by Casey Meyers
- *Walking for Fitness: Make Every Step Count*, by Nina Barough
- *Women's Complete Guide to Walking*, by Jeff Galloway

PROGRAM MODEL **Run Club**

This is an upbeat program which targets new runners or encourages socializing between existing runners, building community and modeling healthy fitness practices in your library.

Advance Planning

STEP 1. Figure out who you are trying to target with this program and what time of day you are going to offer it. Many runners like to run in the early mornings before work. Decide if you want to start your day at 6 a.m. By the

FIGURE 6.4
Run Club poster

afternoon most people are too busy to run. Noon is a good time for day-workers looking to get some exercise on their lunch break, but make sure the run is short enough that they have time to eat something and get back to the office.

FIGURE 6.5 Run Club

Also, having a public shower available in your facility is a bonus, and most of our libraries don't have this. A lot of people don't want to get sweaty and then put back on a power suit. We've had the most success with evening runs (7:00–8:00 p.m.), since that gives people time to get home from work, get changed, have a bite, and arrange for a sitter before going for the run. Depending on where you live, it might be too dark, cold, or unsafe to run at night. Weekends are best for workshops and events, such as a Fun Run or a Dash n' Dine. Will this be an ongoing program, or is there a set beginning and end with a goal?

STEP 2. Find volunteers and/or staff members who are willing to lead this program. Remember that not everyone is going to want to run for thirty minutes and then put their work clothes back on without a shower; you should schedule and choose accordingly. At my library I lead the Thursday night Fun Run at 7:00 p.m. because we close at 8:00 p.m., and so I can go home and shower right after. A volunteer leads the 8:30 a.m. Saturday Fun Run because I don't want to hustle that early in the morning or spend all day smelling funky. If you don't care (or don't mind a sponge bath in the staff washroom), more power to ya!

STEP 3. Map out a route. At my library we usually do a 5-kilometer loop, which takes about thirty-two minutes at a moderate pace, but I schedule an hour for the program because sometimes we are late getting started or some people run slower and we stick together as a group. Faster runners will run back and forth to check on the people in the back.

STEP 4. Decide if this is going to require pre-registration or if it is a drop-in program (ours is drop-in, but workshops or a Couch-to-5-Kilometer run work better with a sign-up). Advertise. We use social media, posters, radio call-in, a web calendar, a paper calendar, and word of mouth. Share to groups that may be interested (local run groups, local sports teams, fitness/health groups, etc.).

Variations

❱ **Trail Runners.** This program involves running on local nature trails instead of the streets.

❱ **Speed Club.** This is a running club that is focused on interval training, hill repeats, fartlek (fast running intermixed with slow running), and so on.

❱ **Couch-to-5-Kilometer.** This is a beginner running program that combines running and walking to get people ready to run their first 5-kilometer run.

❱ **Dash n' Dine.** This is an early morning run club where you meet at a local diner at the end of the run and tuck into breakfast together—it works best on a Saturday or Sunday.

❱ **Fluffy Runners.** This is what my friend calls her running group for people who are not your typical *Runner's World* cover model but who do want to be fit and healthy. There's a great book by Jayne Williams we have in our collection called *Slow, Fat Triathlete* (2004) that really busts the stereotype that you have to look a certain way to be a legitimate athlete. See chapter 7 below for more information about this program.

❱ **Reading Runners Book Club.** See the sidebar for more ideas about adding a book club to your fitness groups.

Materials Required

❏ Staff or volunteers leading the program need appropriate footwear and outerwear. A reflective vest or clothing and a headlamp are handy for running at night.

❏ Sunglasses and/or a hat.

❏ A cell phone in case there is an emergency.

❏ Other items as needed, depending on the variation of program chosen (stop watch, training logs, etc.).

Andrew Richmond

Name: Andrew Richmond, Library Director

Contact: arichmond@ryepubliclibrary.org

Location: Rye Public Library, Rye, New Hampshire

Claim to Fame: Creator of fitness book clubs

All-Star Programs: Running and Reading Book Club;
Climbing and Reading Book Club

Individual sports like running and cycling have always been part of my life, along with the arts and literature. I've always tried to keep a mind/body balance. Librarianship has offered me a way to combine these interests, and more, in a professional capacity. When Christopher McDougall's book *Born to Run* topped the bestseller list several years ago, I thought about tying a book-club concept to a running group. This concept became the first of many Running and Reading sessions at the Rye Public Library. *Born to Run* was an obvious first reading choice. By dividing the book into sections to read in advance of our meetings, we met for several weeks leading up to a local 5-kilometer road race. With a deeper look at smaller sections of the book, we were able to feature details of culture, food, and so on through an e-mail newsletter between sessions and in taste tests at our discussions. Our group met ready to run, held our discussion, and then we went out for a run. We built our distance and pace toward the target race date. I requested that participants start out with some running experience, and the sessions allowed an opportunity to tune up for the race and an opportunity to progressively reflect on *Born to Run*. Of my participants, several were first-timers at racing as we gathered for the 5-kilometer run, while one also trained throughout our sessions for a marathon.

Since then, Running and Reading has discussed several other great running books in novel and memoir form. Most recently the author Becky Wade joined our group via Skype for the final discussion session of her book *Run the World*.

I have also long enjoyed the mountains and mountain sports. Bringing mountain literature together with an activity group offered another interesting book-club opportunity: Climbing and Reading. While New Hampshire offers some great climbing opportunities in its mountainous northern part, Rye is situated on our

continued on the following page ❯❯❯

⟨⟨⟨ continued from the previous page

short, beautiful, but vertically challenged seacoast. As with most areas in the United States, though, indoor climbing gyms are fairly prolific in New Hampshire these days. Through cooperation with a community youth outdoor program instructor, I arranged instruction and access to a nearby climbing wall. Next came book selection. Mountaineering offers a rich range of well-written books full of high adventure and emotional and philosophical extremes. Our first selection was *Touching the Void* by Joe Simpson, an accessible and popular story of a South American climbing venture with an epic survival element. The book offers an exploration of the depths of human motivation and perseverance in the face of adversity. The story proved motivational for those who found their initial experience with climbing to be a physical challenge.

Again, we divided the book into sections, met ready for the short drive to our climbing venue, and discussed the book—and then we climbed. Breaking one book into multiple sections for discussion requires some diversion from standard one-discussion book groups. While discussion questions are available for many books, care has to be taken to avoid "spoiler" glimpses into future chapters over multiple discussions. Many new questions for the intermediate discussions are also required, but a combination of these with publisher-supplied questions serves to keep discussion going over a longer-term consideration of any book.

As each discussion revealed new aspects of the adventure, the corresponding climbing session progressed through new skills and techniques. Some participants shared their climbing knowledge, while others gained brand-new skills and experiences. We culminated with a venture to a larger and more challenging climbing gym and a final gathering at a nearby pub.

Budget Details

$0

This is a relatively no-cost program, unless you bring in special guests to talk to the group and have to pay them. This is where grants come in handy.

Day of the Event

STEP 1. Meet at your determined location (we leave from the library parking lot). Do a few dynamic stretches to warm up while you are waiting for everyone to arrive. It's a good idea to have at least two staff members or volunteers on the run, one to lead and one to follow up in the rear to make sure no one gets left behind. Make sure everyone is aware of the route and how far you are running.

STEP 2. Run. Or run/walk. No one gets left behind, so you should go at the pace of your slowest runner. This is not a race.

STEP 3. At the end we high-five all around, and we take a group selfie to post to the library's Facebook page and the local running group's page to show off how awesome we are. These photos become very inspirational as before-and-after records if you are leading a group of Couch-to-5-Kers or a running-for-weight-loss group.

Tips

1. Run your planned route ahead of time in order to get an idea of any potential problems (busy intersections, uneven terrain that might affect strollers, etc.) and to get a rough estimate of how long it takes to run it at an average pace. Remember that your pace might not be average for your demographic, and plan accordingly.

2. Don't leave anyone behind. Ever. If someone is sick, tired, winded, discouraged, or needs to find a bathroom, stay with them. Be mindful and be patient. Avoid being concerned with your own fitness goals or "making good time."

3. Have a contingency plan if the weather is poor. How will you notify the group if the Run Club is canceled? Do you have an indoor venue nearby you could use instead, like a track?

4. Partner with your local running group or other organizations (perhaps specific to your targeted demographic) to recruit volunteers or help spread the word.

5. Offer periodic workshops or group events to keep morale up and encourage one another. Plan to travel together to local races. Host local events together, such as a Reindeer Run, to raise money for charity. Here are some workshop ideas that have worked at other libraries: ChiRunning/ChiWalking, Ultimate Marathons, Nutrition for Runners, Yoga for Runners, Ironman/Triathlon Training, Foam Rolling for Runners, Pilates for Runners, Gait Clinic, and Posture Clinic.

Multiple Literacy Tie-In

Here are some fun ideas for how you can keep the program moving.

❭ Local maps; books about community parks, trails, or local hikes. For example:

○ *Rail-Trails Michigan and Wisconsin,* by the Rails-to-Trails Conservatory

○ *Trail Running—Chamonix and the Mont Blanc Region,* by Kingsley Jones

○ *Trail Running Western Massachusetts,* by Ben Kimball

❭ Travel books centered on running destinations and experiences. Here are some examples:

○ *Born to Run: A Hidden Tribe, Superathletes, and the Greatest Race the World Has Never Seen,* by Christopher McDougall

○ *The Coolest Race on Earth: Mud, Madmen, Glaciers, and Grannies at the Antarctica Marathon,* by John Hanc

○ *Natural Born Heroes: Mastering the Lost Secrets of Strength and Endurance,* by Christopher McDougall

○ *Run the World: My 3,500-Mile Journey through Running Cultures around the Globe,* by Becky Wade

○ *Running the Seven Continents: Tales of Travel and the Marathon,* by Clint Morrison

○ *The Way of the Runner: A Journey into the Fabled World of Japanese Running,* by Adharanand Finn

❭ Running memoirs (believe it or not, there is an abundance of these). For example:

○ *Confessions of an Unlikely Runner: A Guide to Racing and Obstacle Courses for the Averagely Fit and Halfway Dedicated,* by Dana L. Ayers

○ *Eat and Run: My Unlikely Journey to Ultramarathon Greatness,* by Scott Jurek and Steve Friedman

○ *Finding Ultra: Rejecting Middle Age, Becoming One of the World's Fittest Men, and Discovering Myself,* by Rich Roll

○ *First Ladies of Running: 22 Inspiring Profiles of the Rebels, Rule Breakers, and Visionaries Who Changed the Sport Forever,* by Amby Burfoot

○ *Pre: The Story of America's Greatest Running Legend, Steve Prefontaine,* by Tom Jordon

○ *Running Man: A Memoir,* by Charlie Engle

○ *Ultramarathon Man: Confessions of an All-Night Runner,* by Dean Karnazes
What I Talk About When I Talk About Running: A Memoir, by Haruki Murakami

❭ How-to running books, such as:

○ *Build Your Running Body: A Total-Body Fitness Plan for All Distance Runners, from Milers to Ultramarathoners—Run Farther, Faster, and Injury-Free*, by Peter Magill et al.

○ *ChiRunning: A Revolutionary Approach to Effortless, Injury-Free Running*, by Danny Dreyer and Katherine Dreyer

○ *80/20 Running: Run Stronger and Race Faster by Training Slower*, by Matt Fitzgerald

○ *Older, Faster, Stronger: What Women Runners Can Teach Us All about Living Younger, Longer*, by Margaret Webb

○ *Ready to Run: Unlocking Your Potential to Run Naturally*, by Kelly Starrett and T. J. Murphy

○ *Runner's World Run Less, Run Faster: Become a Faster, Stronger Runner with the Revolutionary 3-Run-a-Week Training Program* (paperback), by Bill Pierce, Scott Murr, and Ray Moss

○ *Running with the Mind of Meditation: Lessons for Training Body and Mind*, by Sakyong Mipham

○ *The Running Revolution: How to Run Faster, Farther, and Injury-Free—for Life*, by Nicholas Romanov and Kurt Bungardt

○ *The Ultimate Beginners Running Guide: The Key to Running Inspired*, by Robert Ryan

❭ Running-related cookbooks. Examples:

○ *The Endurance Training Diet & Cookbook: The How, When, and What for Fueling Runners and Triathletes to Improve Performance*, by Jesse Kropelnicki

○ *The No Meat Athlete Cookbook: Whole Food, Plant-Based Recipes to Fuel Your Workouts—and the Rest of Your Life*, by Matt Frazier, Stepfanie Romine, and Rich Roll

○ *Racing Weight Cookbook: Lean, Light Recipes for Athletes*, by Matt Fitzgerald and Georgie Fear

○ *Run Fast, Eat Slow: Nourishing Recipes for Athletes*, by Shalene Flanagan and Elyse Kopecky

○ *The Runner's World Cookbook: 150 Ultimate Recipes for Fueling Up and Slimming Down—While Enjoying Every Bite*, by Joanna Sayago Golub and Deena Castor

○ *The Runner's World Meals on the Run: 150 Energy-Packed Recipes in 30 Minutes or Less*, by Joanna Sayago Golub

❭ General fitness books; stretching/yoga for runners books or DVDs. Examples:

○ *Becoming a Supple Leopard: The Ultimate Guide to Resolving Pain, Preventing Injury, and Optimizing Athletic Performance*, by Kelly Starrett and Glen Cordoza

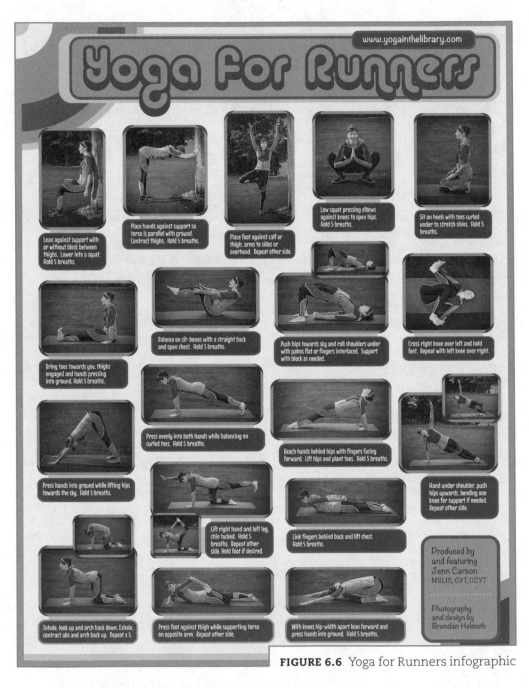

FIGURE 6.6 Yoga for Runners infographic

- *Gaiam Athletic Yoga: Yoga for Runners*, DVD (2015)
- *Hit Reset: Revolutionary Yoga for Athletes*, by Erin Taylor
- *The Maffetone Method: The Holistic, Low-Stress, No-Pain Way to Exceptional Fitness*, by Philip Maffetone
- *Yoga for Runners*, by Christine Felstead

❭ Try adding some stretching to the program, or at least giving them a hand-out of stretches to take home (and maybe a book or two from your display). You can download the infographic in figure 6.6 in PDF format at www.jenn-carson.com/resources.html.

PROGRAM MODEL Roll with Us! Foam Rolling Workshop

Foam rolling is a self-myofascial release (SMR) technique that is used by athletes and physical therapists to stretch, lengthen, and relax muscles. It is easy to do, using simple exercises and equipment (sometime even things you can find around the house—like tennis balls).

FIGURE 6.7
Foam Rolling poster

Advance Planning

STEP 1. Find a volunteer (physio-therapists, yoga teachers, fitness inst-ructors, or occupational therapists are often certified in this technique) or staff member who can provide the workshop. You can learn a lot about self-massage techniques from reading Dr. Kelly Starrett's two great books: *Becoming a Supple Leopard* and *Deskbound*.

STEP 2. Buy any foam rollers, lacrosse balls, or other equipment you will need. Or find out if you can borrow some from a local gym. Or perhaps the facilitator will bring their own. You could also ask participants to bring a ten-nis ball (or other item, depending on what you are teaching) from home. Wellness grants are sometimes available to cover the costs of materials.

STEP 3. Pick a day and time. We offered this program over the course of two Saturdays, with one focusing on the upper body and one on the lower body. Each session lasted two hours.

STEP 4. You'll probably want to do a pre-registration for this program so you know in advance how much equipment you'll need. Advertise. We use social media, posters, radio call-in, a web calendar, a paper calendar, and

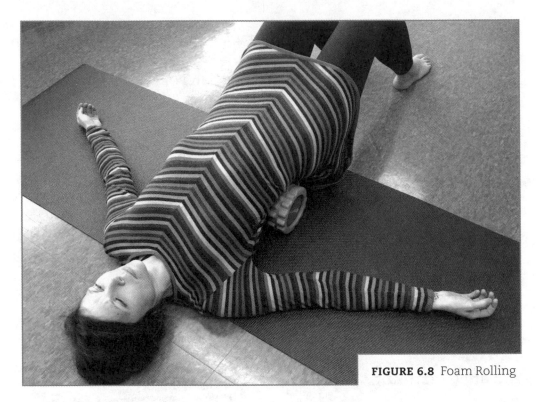

FIGURE 6.8 Foam Rolling

word of mouth. Share to groups that may be interested (local fitness groups, runners, yoga studios, doctor's offices, etc.).

Variations

》 *Feldenkrais Method workshop.* If you have a practitioner of this method in your area, see if they'll come in for a talk.

》 *Acupuncture Clinic.* We had great success getting a local acupuncturist to give a talk about Chinese medicine, and he even delivered treatments on a few brave volunteers. Check with your insurance and local regulations to see if this is feasible.

》 *Gait or Posture Clinic.* Have someone from the kinesiology department at your local university or a running expert come in and give a posture or gait clinic. They can monitor your movements, running/walking gait (figure 6.9), and standing position in order to recommend exercises you can do to correct imbalances.

》 *Yoga/Stretching for Runners.* You can find a program handout for this at the Jenn Carson website: www.jenncarson.com/resources.html.

FIGURE 6.9 Gait Clinic

Materials Required

The good news is that this workshop can be done wearing pretty much any sort of casual clothing and you don't need shoes. Depending on what exercises you (or your facilitator) are teaching, you may want to buy or borrow any of the following (see the "Budget Details" section for cheapo do-it-yourself versions):

- ❏ Lacrosse or tennis balls
- ❏ Battlestar rollers (if you can afford them—they are awesome!)
- ❏ Foam rollers of varying density and size
- ❏ Resistance bands
- ❏ Yoga mats
- ❏ Liability waivers
- ❏ Evaluation forms

Budget Details

$100–500+

This one could get pricey, but there are ways to cut costs. If you can recruit a volunteer or a trained staff member to teach, that would save you the $50-$200+ for a facilitator. You could borrow the equipment from a local gym

or yoga studio, or see if your teacher can provide them. If not, consider investing in 10–15 foam rollers and having them as an alternative format collection.
Another possibility is applying for a wellness grant to cover the cost of the rollers, and letting the students take them home at the end (that's what we did).
Another alternative is using cheap, household items you can get at a thrift or
dollar store, like pool noodles, water bottles, rolling pins, tennis balls (in tube
socks so they don't roll away), pantyhose (in place of resistance bands), and
even marshmallows (put them between your toes to stretch them out—consume them afterwards at your own ick-tolerance!). I've even used wooden
dowels from the hardware store and balls from the pet shop in a pinch.

Day of the Event

STEP 1. Gather all the supplies you will be using and set up a yoga mat
with all the necessary props for each person who has signed up. Once your
facilitator arrives, greet them and ask what they need. They may be bringing
props, depending on the agreement you've worked out.

STEP 2. Prepare a clipboard with the liability waivers and greet guests at
the door.

STEP 3. Class begins. If you are teaching, some great places to get lesson
plans from are Kelly Starrett's previously mentioned books or his YouTube
videos.

STEP 4. Clean up after class. Hand out the evaluation forms, if using, or
solicit verbal feedback.

Tips

1. If feedback from the first class is positive, consider adding it as a regular
weekly program, if you can secure a facilitator. While taking a class once is
nice, self-care bodywork, like yoga, is something that people benefit from
doing on a regular basis. Consider handing out lists of the exercises so people
can practice at home, or even better, have some books or videos handy that
they can check out.

2. You might want to have some baby-wipes on hand to clean off the tools
afterwards, for good hygiene. Alcohol wipes might hurt the plastic surfaces;
check with your teacher or the package your tools came in. An environmentally
friendly option is vinegar and water, but then your library might smell for a bit.

3. If you or your patrons have long hair, I suggest tying it up. Getting hair trapped between a foam roller and the floor, or between a lacrosse ball and your bare skin, hurts.

Multiple Literacy Tie-In

Here are some display ideas for participants to browse (use multiple formats—audio, text, braille, DVDs, etc.), and which will encourage them to try the techniques they learned at home.

❱ Books or instructional DVDs about foam rolling, massage techniques, reflexology, yoga, Pilates, stretching, or ergonomics. Here are some examples:

- *Becoming a Supple Leopard, 2nd Edition: The Ultimate Guide to Resolving Pain, Preventing Injury, and Optimizing Athletic Performance,* by Kelly Starrett and Glen Cordoza
- *Deskbound: Standing Up to a Sitting World,* by Kelly Starrett and Glen Cordoza
- *Don't Just Sit There,* by Katy Bowman
- *Foam Rolling: 50 Exercises for Massage, Injury Prevention, and Core Strength,* by Karina Inkstar
- *Foam Rolling: Relieve Pain—Prevent Injury—Improve Mobility,* by Sam Woodworth
- *Human Factors and Ergonomics in Practice: Improving System Performance and Human Well-Being in the Real World,* by Steven Shorrock and Claire Williams
- *The Practice of Natural Movement: Reclaim Power, Health, and Freedom,* by Erwan Le Corre
- *The Roll Model: A Step-by-Step Guide to Erase Pain, Improve Mobility, and Live Better in Your Body,* by Jill Miller
- *Total Foam Rolling Techniques: Trade Secrets of a Personal Trainer,* by Steve Barrett

❱ Books or DVDs on recovering from injuries, such as:

- *Gift of Injury,* by Stuart McGill and Brian Carroll
- *The Knee Crisis Handbook: Understanding Pain, Preventing Trauma, Recovering from Injury, and Building Healthy Knees for Life,* by Brian Halpern and Laura Tucker
- *The MELT Method: A Breakthrough Self-Treatment System to Eliminate Chronic Pain, Erase the Signs of Aging, and Feel Fantastic in Just 10 Minutes a Day,* by Sue Hitzmann

○ *Pain-Free Posture Handbook: 40 Dynamic, Easy Exercises to Look and Feel Your Best*, by Laura Pavilak and Nikki Alstedter

○ *Simple Steps to Foot Pain Relief: The New Science of Healthy Feet*, by Katy Bowman

FIGURE 6.10
Ballroom Dancing poster

PROGRAM MODEL
Ballroom Dancing

There's nothing more romantic than seeing smiling couples waltzing through stacks of books. Consider hosting a ballroom dance program in your library—it will be very popular, I promise!

Advance Planning

STEP 1. Pick a good time to have the program. You really need to set aside at least five or six one-hour sessions, since it takes quite a while to learn the steps. I don't know what it's like in January or February where you live, but here in Woodstock it is cold and dark, and everyone seems to be hibernating. When they do venture out to get essential supplies (like books!), there is a lot of complaining about the weather. In these long months of winter, when there are only eight or nine hours of light per day and the temperature dips 20 or 30 degrees below freezing, our patrons are desperately looking for fun things to do indoors—and they like it even better if it involves some much-needed exercise. This is when we first offered the Ballroom Dancing program, during the fall and winter. It became so popular we even added a spring session. Remember to be flexible, since you will have to work with the instructor to see when he or she is available.

STEP 2. Find a teacher (unless you have someone on staff who is qualified). Ask them if they are available for the dates you were thinking about. I was really lucky: I asked around town and found the name of a local teacher, Deborah Helle, who said that she wasn't currently teaching but would love to, and was willing to do it for free if I could get some couples interested. Find out

FIGURE 6.11 Ballroom Dance Stacks

from your instructor what sort of dance he or she will be teaching so you can answer any questions people calling to register might have. We offer foxtrot, waltz, tango, swing, and more.

STEP 3. Decide if you will only take couples or if singles are welcome to come too. If you are worried about patrons being creepy, accepting singles might not be a

FIGURE 6.12
Ballroom Dance couple

great idea. You know your patrons best. Pre-registration is required for this program, unless you have a gymnasium, a loudspeaker system, and multiple teachers with helpers. Four or five couples is manageable.

STEP 4. Book the room. You want something large, open, and preferably with no posts in the middle of the room.

STEP 5. Advertise. After we settled on some dates for a six-week program, we decided to do a preliminary post on Facebook to see who might be interested. Due to the size of the room, we could only take four couples. By the end of the day, our sign-up sheet was full, and by the end of the week we had over 8,000 views on Facebook (not bad for a town with a population of just over 5,000).

Jessica Jupitus

Name: Jessica Jupitus, Public Services Manager

Contact: jjupitus@saclibrary.org

Location: Sacramento Public Library

Claim to Fame: Alternative fitness classes such as Punk Rock Aerobics, Alterna-Pilates, Bollyrobics, Brutal Yoga, Come Out! for Aerobics, Glam Metal Yoga, Hench as ****, Holidaze Yoga, Industrial Strength, Partner Yoga, Riot Grrl Plyo, and Zombie Survival Aerobics.

All-Star Program: Punk Rock Aerobics.

As a former skater and coach for the local roller derby league, staying fit and active is incredibly important to me. I enjoy punk music, movement, and surprising people with what their library can do, so I combined all three of these options into my very first Punk Rock Aerobics. I was inspired by the book of the same name by Hilken Mancini and Maura Jasper. My first priority was to create a playlist of appropriate music. You can use free streaming services, or the CDs in your library's collection, or whatever works best for you. I compiled my favorite Dead Kennedys/Misfits/Bad Religion songs into a 55-minute playlist. I shifted the songs around so the beats matched the intensity of the moves I was planning, including a warm-up and a cool-down. I used library resources extensively to construct a total body workout that was scalable in difficulty to ensure that folks at all levels of fitness could participate. I worked with our legal counsel to get a liability waiver just to be sure the library was protected in case of accidental injury. We advertised on our various media outlets and I promoted the program personally, since word of mouth is usually the best way to share. With a title like Punk Rock Aerobics, it quickly got picked up by local newspapers. We averaged between 20 and 40 adult attendees for each event and ran it monthly for nearly two years. We got skaters, we got library fans, and most thrillingly, we got people who had never been in a library before to come in and try something new. Gyms can be intimidating to people, but everyone is welcome in the library, and this means that library staff are uniquely positioned to be a gateway to all sorts of new experiences.

Make it happen. You've prepared the playlist (about 53–59 minutes of music), you've written the workout (matching the moves to the songs and including both a warm-up and a cool-down), you've promoted your face off, you have the waivers printed and ready to be signed—what now? Empty out your community room. Be sure that no flailing limb will whack into a stray chair. Set up your laptop and speakers (I use these) and make sure you can stream your music, that the Wi-Fi is connected, and that the music is loud enough to hear, but also soft enough for the dancers to hear *you*. Dress the part. Wear your theme gear—I have an autographed (by Jerry Only of the Misfits) denim vest with punk pins all over it that I wear for Punk Rock Aerobics. Provide water. If you don't have a drinking fountain nearby, buy mini-bottles of water. I always encourage people to bring their own, but they always forget. Finally, have fun. People love subverting the paradigm of library behavior, and they are primed to like whatever it is you are going to do. If you mess up a move, skip it.

STEP 6. Plan the music. Will the instructor expect the music to be provided? Or will the instructor bring it? Will the instructor need a device to play the music on?

Variations

) *Family Ballroom Dance.* If you thought couples dancing was sweet, try a room full of kids dancing with each other, or daughters standing on daddy's toes. We offered a ballroom dance lesson last year at our annual Christmas event and it was a big hit.

) *Zumba.* This program is very popular in many libraries; why not try it in yours?

) *Belly Dance.* Our instructor also teaches belly dance classes, and these are fun and challenging.

) *Pole Dancing Classes.* Google "pole dancing classes library" if you don't believe this is a real thing.

) *Punk Rock Aerobics.* Are you looking to offer something less traditional than the schmaltzy waltz? See the sidebar for more information.

Materials Required

❏ Liability waivers
❏ Photo releases

❑ Evaluation forms
❑ Music and something to play it on

Budget Details

$20–500+

If you are lucky enough to find a volunteer instructor who brings her own Bluetooth speaker and iPod, you call pull this program off for free. If that's the case, you should at least splurge on a little thank-you gift for the instructor. Otherwise an instructor could cost you $100 per session or more, depending on their qualifications and where you live.

Day of the Event

STEP 1. Empty the room of all tables, but maybe set up a few chairs around the edges in case people need to sit for a break or to put their dancing shoes on.

STEP 2. Greet your instructor and test the music to make sure it is working.

STEP 3. Have the liability waivers on a clipboard and greet your guests at the door. Also have them sign a photo release if you plan on taking photos (and you should—they are so fun to share on social media—dancing at the library!)

STEP 4. Enjoy watching the couples dance, and get the instructor water or anything else he or she needs.

STEP 5. Thank everyone for coming, and if this is the last week of the session, hand out evaluation forms.

Tips

1. Consider whether you want an age limit for this program. The couples from our town were all ages, from skittish newlyweds to retired lovebirds. We even had a mother ask if she could bring her teenage daughters and take turns dancing with them so they could learn—sure, no problem! Our general rule is sixteen and up, but we make exceptions.

2. Consider whether you will allow singles. We do, and one of our staff members volunteers to come in on his day off to be the instructor's helper.

She uses him to demonstrate the dance steps, and he's also there to dance with anyone who came alone. It's a nice option for people who are uncoupled or in a relationship with someone who isn't interested, able, or available to dance.

3. If you have security in the building, it might not be a bad idea to have them present. Tempers can get testy when people are learning something new in front of an audience and I've seen a few squabbles, though nothing that involved anyone in uniform getting into the mix. Security might also discourage those who may be extra *handsy* with their partners.

4. Consider whether staff should be involved. We have one staff member who helps out the instructor, as I mentioned, but he comes in and volunteers on his own time. He feels fine about it and I don't get involved, since he's not on the clock. Check with your boss, administration, public policies, and possibly human resources to see whether or not staff should be in such close proximity to patrons. I attended one of the ballroom dance sessions once, but I came on my own time and brought a date, and didn't dance with anyone else. To avoid weirdness with patrons, I'd advise against dancing with them.

5. Buy your instructor a really nice thank-you gift (especially if the instructor is doing this for free). Teaching dance is hard. I usually give Deborah a beautiful bouquet of flowers or a gift card to a local restaurant after a six-week session.

6. Be prepared to offer more Ballroom Dancing programs. The first program was so popular that our waiting list swelled to over forty people, and our phone rang constantly. It has become a regular program in our rotation and we now offer it three or four times a year. In fact, Deborah started traveling to two nearby library branches and offering it there to keep up with the demand!

Multiple Literacy Tie-In

Create some eye-catching displays to encourage dancers to whip out their library card and shimmy their way to the circulation desk:

❱ Ballroom dance movies. Participants are going to want to see their new skills in action:

- *Ballroom Dancer* (2011)
- *Dance with Me* (1998)
- *Dirty Dancing* (1987)

- *Grease* (1978)
- *Mad Hot Ballroom* (2005)
- *Shall We Dance?* (2004)
- *Silver Linings Playbook* (2012)
- *Strictly Ballroom* (1992)
- *Take the Lead* (2006)

❱ Dance music. Your dancers are going to need something to practice with at home. Here are a few suggestions:

- *Ballroom Dance Music*, by Swiss Ballroom Orchestra
- *Dance with Me Soundtrack*, by Michael Convertino
- *Dances!* by Ô-Celli
- *Come Dance with Me: Ballroom Favorites*, by 101 Strings Orchestra
- *Rumba*, by Gold Star Ballroom
- *Shall We Dance?* by Andre Rieu

Note

1. You can see an example of a labyrinth mat at https://www.labyrinthcompany.com/collections/poly-canvas-mats.

Inclusive Movement
Involving Special Populations through Outreach and Inreach

Without community, or other people to relate to, we don't have a sense of being real. We know that the more social contacts people have, the happier, more optimistic and healthier they are. Our strongest ties are those relationships characterized by frequent contact, deep feelings of affection and obligation, and a broad base of understanding. Strong ties tend to buffer people from life's stresses and lead to better social and psychological safety.

—*Carla Hannaford*

I returned to library work after the birth of my second son and took on the dynamic role of supervising the bookmobile for the southwest region of our province. While I didn't get the opportunity to do many movement-based programs on the bus, I started teaching weekly fifteen-minute "yoga breaks" to the staff at our regional office—deskbound technicians and members of the administration. Their ages ranged from the late twenties to the early seventies, and their fitness levels ranged from the very fit (triathletes and hockey players) to the very, very unfit (multiple chronic conditions). I adapted the gentler yoga classes to fit everyone's needs the best I could. After several months of classes, I administered a survey (see figure 7.1) to get some feedback on how everyone was feeling. The results were so positive that I started getting asked to lead a yoga break at every management meeting or staff training I attended. At this time I also gave an Ignite Talk on "Yoga in the Library:

Outreach and Inreach" at the Atlantic Provinces Library Association Conference. I trained the staff of the children's department at our resource center on how to deliver yoga programs to children. I was still working away at my MSLIS degree, and I developed an independent study called "Kinesthetic Applications in Library Programming" under Dr. Denise Agosto, who would become my mentor in all things related to youth services. My major project was to develop my website www.yogainthelibrary.com as a resource for library staff who were interested in running yoga and meditation programs in their libraries, or for those interested in collection development on the topic. Years later, the website is still regularly updated, and it continues to be a valuable resource for library staff worldwide.

In May 2014, I was invited to work at the New Brunswick College of Craft and Design as their student-life coordinator. While doing the usual jobs of executing major events like convocation and orientation, I also revamped their (mostly nonexistent) extracurricular program department, and I introduced yoga-in-the-studio (where I would go around to each department and deliver program-specific exercises to meet the students' needs and prevent repetitive strain injuries, which are common among craftspeople). I also created a safe-ride partnership with the neighboring university, a food security program that brought healthy farm-fresh produce to the students for free, and a volunteer program where students would be awarded a bursary for points earned working in the library and art gallery. At this time I continued delivering yoga, meditation, and movement-based programs at the big provincial resource library next door and in the college's small, specialized library and art studios. I dug deeper and deeper into my research into kinetics and neurobiology. Now that I was mostly working with young adults and adults, I could really see how a lack of physical literacy training in childhood

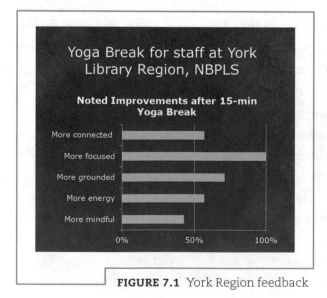

FIGURE 7.1 York Region feedback

could radically affect adult participation in sports or even any kind of movement-based activity.

As we learned in earlier chapters, children are intrinsically motivated to explore and interact with their environment in an almost compulsive fashion. Ideally, this insatiable curiosity and enthusiasm continues into adulthood. Unfortunately, due to a variety of factors, including the overwhelming sense of stress, overwork, and responsibility that most adults feel burdened by, this rarely happens. So offering movement-based library programs that appeal to physically literate patrons is a no-brainer. You say "yoga triathlon" or "Spartan race" within earshot of the right people and you will have a parking lot full of spandexed and sneakered health nuts before the book drop is even emptied in the morning. I know, I'm now one of them. But what about reaching out to the patrons who don't know the difference between CrossFit and a croissant? Or the patrons who don't make the connection between the library as an authoritative (often governmental) agency and the library as a place of fun and wellness? Our relentless exposure to celebrity athletes and extreme sporting events (anyone up for some wingsuit skydiving?) leaves many individuals feeling not only incompetent, but convinced that any progress on their own personal physical-literacy journey will be unworthy of attention or accolades. And we can't forget the great demon of perfectionism. For many of our patrons, if they can't "bend it like Beckham" they don't want to play the game at all.

How do we overcome this reluctance on the part of our patrons, and also perhaps our own staff? As Margaret Whitehead suggests, we can start by offering extrinsic rewards to our less naturally motivated clientele: the possibility of losing weight, praise from coworkers and friends, or a healthy treat afterwards. The goal is to "offer opportunities for success, to nurture interest, and to re-ignite a drive to capitalize on physical potential. Where there is success there can be a return to intrinsic motivation, with individuals becoming self-motivated and no longer reliant on others to spur them into action."[1] We can brainstorm ways to acknowledge when our patrons make even small steps (such as showing up), and we can make sure their progress is celebrated based on their own advancement, and not relative to others. Some of the rewards we offer may come in the form of praise, prizes, refreshments, or certificates of accomplishment, but others may offer a more human acknowledgment. At the end of every yoga class I teach, I have the students come to *savasana* (lying on their backs on the floor, usually with eyes closed) and I come around and give each person a foot and a neck adjustment. Before I begin, I give them the option to (anonymously, because their eyes are closed) put their hands on their bellies if they don't wish to be touched (it's very important to always have an opt-out; you never know who has experienced trauma or has negative personal feelings about being touched by a relative stranger). Some teachers give out cards (figure 7.2) at the beginning of class that students can use to alert the teacher to whether they want assists or not.[2] Many students over the years have told me that this is their favorite part of the practice—this chance to be touched in a calming, nonsexual way and to just *be* on their mats, without being expected to do anything, or *be* anyone. They only need to breathe.

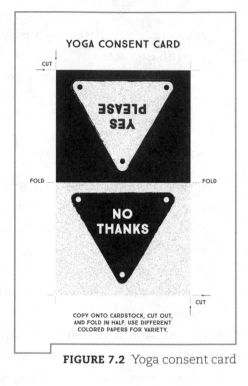

FIGURE 7.2 Yoga consent card

Targeting Specific Populations—The Outreach

How do you reach the people in your community who you feel can best be helped by movement-based programs, but who are also the least likely to come, for myriad reasons? Try making a list of your target audience. Mine might look something like this (yours may be entirely different):

⟩ Seniors
⟩ People with disabilities, chronic conditions, or other physical and mental barriers to exercise
⟩ People who cannot afford gym memberships or pay for classes, for themselves or their children
⟩ People in our First Nation or Indigenous communities
⟩ My own staff

Once you've got your list, then you need to focus on reaching out to these groups. This usually means visiting them where they are and tailoring your marketing and program delivery to appeal to their needs and interests. Let me tell you a little tale of how I learned this the hard way.

The Story of "The Fluffy Runners"

As you've seen in previous chapters, I am an avid runner, and I sit on the board of a local running group that also partners with my library to host a wide variety of events. Three times a week we hold a 5-kilometer fun run, but one of our hardest challenges is getting beginner runners to join us. For months I worried that they saw our sweaty, smiling faces and lean bodies on posters and social media pictures and thought, "No way! Not for me!" My friend Aynslie, who is also a member of our local run club and a regular library patron, created her own splinter group called "The Fluffy Runners." She wanted to get back into running and wanted other people to train with who "looked like her."[3] I didn't see why it mattered that I was lean, and the other regular runners in the library running group were slim too. I took this personally. I didn't understand why my friend didn't want to run with us. But instead of asking, or trying to have empathy, I pouted and said nothing. Runners are often fairly introverted individuals (or else they wouldn't amble along solo for miles), but we all have a deep need for human connection, especially if we are prone to long bouts of introspection or have isolating jobs or hobbies. Sometimes if we have someone waiting on our doorstep at 6 a.m., we're more likely to be motivated to get out there on a cold January morning instead of hitting the snooze button. I understood why Aynslie wanted to run with others, but I didn't understand why she needed her own group.

Aynslie's "Fluffy Runners" met and ran at different times than ours, something that worked with their schedules, but we all showed up at the same community races. I even held a program at the library, at their request, to teach them proper warm-ups and stretching (always do dynamic warm-ups before a run, and long holds after the run). But it gave me pause that I couldn't seem to attract these newbie runners to *our* group even though they were running the same distances we were (and sometimes even the same route). There were overweight and even obese runners coming to our workshops on form, nutrition, and yoga, and they were coming to our yearly family runs and races, so they were clearly motivated and moving, but they didn't seem to want to run with us in training. Why? Where was I going wrong? I felt terrible.

Let's talk for a few minutes about obesity, which is a delicate subject and one you will have to address if you're going to offer movement-based programs in your library. Let me be clear that I support the notion that everyone has a right to do whatever they want with their own body, provided they aren't hurting anyone else. Some people argue that being intensely overweight puts a great deal of strain on the body and it is therefore a form of slow suicide. I've known and loved many people with obese bodies in my life, and very few of them *actively chose* to be overweight. According to Statistics Canada, 54 percent of people over the age of eighteen are considered overweight or obese based on the body mass index.[4] The numbers are even worse in the United States, with a staggering 70 percent of men and women reported as being obese or overweight.[5] This is not a new discovery; the World Health Organization has been warning people about the global obesity epidemic since the 1990s, and we are now starting to see the devastating effects of what is essentially a mostly preventable disease.[6] And yes, it *is* a disease, according to the American and Canadian Medical Associations.[7] Don't assume that overweight people are complacent or lazy. Some got that way through the side effects of medication or other health issues. Also, many people are struggling very, very hard to try to change lifelong habits and coping mechanisms, and the first step is accepting them as they are today and acknowledging those efforts. The truth is, you will have patrons who are very overweight, for a variety of reasons. This is where they are today. The effects of being overweight are not just physical but emotional. Children who are teased or bullied because they are overweight have lower self-esteem and are often excluded socially.[8] Diez (1998) has created a list of the terrible consequences of childhood obesity that extend into adulthood:

❱ They are ranked by other children as less likeable
❱ They experience decreased acceptance rates for college
❱ They are considered less desirable by employers
❱ They are often in a lower socioeconomic class
❱ They are frequently teased by peers and so they develop friendships with younger children, or with no one at all, hampering their social skills
❱ They have difficulty finding clothes that fit properly or are the latest fashion

❯ They suffer from others overestimating their age because of their size (and/or early sexual development), and so people expect more adult behavior from them

❯ They often have a distorted body image[9]

Clearly, with all these consequences and the rate of obesity in our population, it is imperative that libraries do something to support their patrons. Keeping in mind what we have learned about how children's or adults' perceptions of themselves and their own abilities may greatly impact their participation, how do we go about creating a safe and welcoming environment where they feel comfortable and empowered to join in the fun?

The United Kingdom's National Institute of Health and Clinical Excellence provides a helpful list of things that health workers can do to prevent and mitigate the effect of obesity in adults and children.[10] Many of these strategies can be employed by libraries, which, unlike some other service providers, can offer them free of charge:

❯ Providing a supportive and motivating environment

❯ Promoting family involvement

❯ Dietary education and advice

❯ Opportunities for regular activity and structured exercise programs

❯ Programs delivered by trained professionals

❯ Long-term support

I already know that most of you are offering an inclusive and hospitable environment because you are librarians and it is part of our mandate. Public libraries can offer family programs (see chapter 4 for examples) both on-site and out in the community. We can invite local wellness and nutrition experts to give talks at our facilities, and we can provide materials in multiple formats that touch on these topics. If your library has a books-by-mail program or provides interlibrary loans, make sure to promote your wellness collection in as many venues as possible. We can provide long-term support by ensuring that we offer movement-based and wellness programming all year long and not just around the New Year when everyone is diet-crazy, or during the summer reading club when we have more staff and traffic.

Recent studies have shown that involving children in exercise programs significantly increases children's resilience to bullying and prevents suicide.

Regular exercise lowers suicide attempts and ideation in teens by 23 percent.[11] Children who exercise regularly are healthier, stronger, and less likely to appear physically weak to their peers. Exercise also increases self-confidence, which makes a child less vulnerable to being picked on in the first place and more likely to stand up for himself and report the bullying, if it does happen. Exercise also releases the pent-up anger and shame that often leads children to be bullies in the first place. Bullying doesn't just happen among children and teens. Spend an hour in any locker room, army barracks, hospital waiting room, or online comments thread and you'll be nauseated at the things people do and say to one another. By providing a no-trash-talk environment (about anyone, including yourself), you can provide a place to foster strong friendships and bonding through shared experience. I've been fortunate enough to make a number of long-term friendships from my local running group, Brazilian Jiu Jitsu club, and yoga studio. The number-one insulator against victimization is having a close friend whom you can confide in and who normalizes you among your peer group. Social isolation is the worst thing for both bullies and the bullied. Library programs that occur on a daily, weekly, or monthly basis encourage children and teens to create these pair bonds outside of their regular school-day environment, and for adults outside of their workplaces, and for seniors outside of their homes. Having a place where patrons can operate outside of their existing entrenched social roles can be very liberating. You may be surprised to see a normally shy and withdrawn patron suddenly open up and become a group leader when given the tools and opportunity.

When you are under stress (figure 7.3), your fight-or-flight system kicks in, your digestion slows or stops, your immune system is suppressed, and your body is flooded with cortisol and adrenaline. This is great if you are being chased by a bear or you're escaping from a burning building, but your poor parasympathetic nervous system can only take so much stress before you see long-term impacts. If a child or adult is experiencing daily stressors, either at school, work, or home, the effects can be devastating. The good news is that exercise can "reset" the nervous system, quickly bringing our body back into the relaxation and recovery phase. Anyone who has experienced the deep calm, satisfaction, and elation felt after a yoga class, a good run, or a game of pick-up knows this firsthand. As planners and facilitators, we must focus on intrinsic motivation factors such as excitement, accomplishment, and pushing

FIGURE 7.3 Stress

to our patrons' skill edge, rather than just extrinsic factors such as pleasing others, losing weight, or getting a reward.[12] We may pull people in with the promise of rewards (Free food! Free yoga class!), but we keep them coming back by the healthy feelings of belonging and improved self-esteem that we engender together. By giving patrons the opportunity to enjoy themselves while being active, we can mitigate the impact of bullying and negative media portrayals of overweight people, even if we can't always prevent these things.

So, back to my story. Given the list from the National Institute of Health and Clinical Excellence, I thought we were hitting all the marks—so why wouldn't "The Fluffy Runners" join us for our thrice-weekly fun runs if they were going the same distance anyway? I finally swallowed my pride and asked Aynslie, "What made you decide to start a 'fluffy runners' group?" Here's her reply:

> In the fall of 2016, I was hearing stories of women wanting to learn how to run but were too intimidated to join the local running club or Couch to 5K training group. There is nothing intimidating about these groups, but when you have a low self-esteem, you avoid anything that you perceive may be tough. These women, myself included, were either overweight, out-of-shape, or both. I had started running to deal with my depression and anxiety, and I knew it was an excellent way to be fit both mentally and physically. I decided to create a running group for these women named the Fluffy Runners.

A friend of mine has a Facebook page named "Fairly Healthy Recipes for Fluffy People." I really resonated to the word "fluffy" because it is another word for overweight or out-of-shape persons, but it also means friendly, cozy, loveable, and huggable. It was important for me to give these women more self-esteem, along with a healthier lifestyle. I wanted them to start to love themselves.[13]

After reading this e-mail from Aynslie, I felt much better. It was a great, humbling reminder that the world doesn't revolve around me and my library. My running group wasn't intimidating, but the "Fluffy Runners" *felt* intimidated. It was something they were going through inside themselves. It wasn't because we ran too fast or weren't inclusive enough. Aynslie also told me that they preferred running on the trail to the road, and moreover, the days we ran didn't always work with their schedules. So it was a problem of logistics *and* self-perception. This gave my ego the swift kick in the (spandex) pants it needed and made me remember what I have outlined so strongly in chapter 2—*get feedback*. The River Valley Runners and I had set the days and times for our fun runs based on *our* schedules without asking the greater running community what worked best for them. It was partially our egocentricity and myopia that was causing people to avoid our club, not just self-image barriers.

If I would have just asked Aynslie two years earlier, it would have been two years we could have all been running together. This isn't to discount the fact that yes, some people in your community will feel intimidated attending programs because of their weight or fitness levels, and you can't offer enough programs to fit everyone's schedule. This is regrettable, but you have to accept it. You can't accommodate everyone, and you can't make, cajole, or bribe people into exercising. They have to *want* to come. But you have to *ask* people what they want and how they want it, not just assume they don't want it at all because they aren't engaged. And then you have to really *listen*. This is a hard lesson I have learned.

We now alternate trail and road running. We've moved the running schedule around a bit. I'm working on a program that targets people who are just at the beginning of their fitness journey. I'm actively seeking someone to lead a couch-to-5-kilometer run program who looks, in Aynslie's words, "like her." No matter how much empathy we have, sometimes we just can't put ourselves in another person's shoes. I have no idea what it is like to be transgender, or black, or a new immigrant, or blind, or obese. We need to make sure when we are creating and leading programs, especially programs which ask our patrons to be vulnerable and try something hard and new, that these programs are being led by someone who has gone through a similar experience. I'm also working with the Canadian Mental Health Association to create a monthly Body-Image Bootcamp which will address issues such as realistic goal-setting, disordered eating, media literacy, being healthy at any size, and radical self-care. I'm partnering with a mental health advocate who has personal experience with these topics. This program will last six months and every participant will take home a workbook. It will be free, as always. Stay tuned to my blog on the ALA's Programming Librarian website for details.[14]

Fit After Fifty

Why is it important to offer movement-based programming that targets an older adult population? Sadly, after the age of thirty, muscle mass, endurance, bone density, and flexibility are all lost at about 10 percent per decade.[15] Another worrisome fact is that many people over seventy, especially women, are unable to walk more than a quarter of a mile, restricting their world to a small radius around their home and the distance they can walk from their car.[16] This doesn't mean that fitness can't be improved, even radically, after the age of fifty. In fact, there was a recent book written by Margaret Webb called *Older, Faster, Stronger: What Women Runners Can Teach All of Us about*

FIGURE 7.4
Elderly Ballroom Dance

Living Younger, Longer, in which she explores what it was like to get into the best shape of her life, when she considered herself past her prime.[17] Many of my programs are well-attended by fit seniors, but what about the ones who aren't showing up? How can we reach them?

One way is by offering programs that may be more appealing to those with limited mobility. I've had a lot of success with Chair Yoga and Laughter Yoga programs. We also offer an adult coloring program that is very popular, as well as a weekly International Fiber Enthusiasts Club. These patrons come from both sides of the Canada-U.S. border to knit, weave, crochet, felt, and needle-point together. Sometimes I pop in and teach them yoga for their hands and shoulders to do while they are seated. Gardening programs and cooking programs are also popular. What about trying chi gong or tai chi? Check out the sidebar to learn more.

First Nation Communities

I'm lucky enough to live on the traditional unceded territory of the Wolastoqiyik people, which runs along the banks of the Wulastukw, which translates as "The Beautiful River." The English colonists renamed it the St. John River, which is what it is still commonly called today. To the south of where I live is the Woodstock First Nation (WFN), and to the north, about 45 minutes away, is the Tobique First Nation (TFN). Both of these First Nations belong to the same band (tribe) of Indigenous people, locally known as the Maliseet. I do a lot of outreach work in both communities, which don't have their own public libraries, by partnering with various members in their various organizations. Terri Paul, from WFN, and I have collaborated on a number of art installations and reconciliation projects at the library and local schools.[18] I also had a local First Nation artist come in and teach children in our library how to make traditional deerskin shakers in honor of National Aboriginal Day.[19] I've teamed up with the manager of the Perth-Andover Public Library, which is closer to TFN, and we travel to the community school together to deliver yoga programs and talk about our services for Indigenous people of all ages. In support of the Sisters in Spirit Campaign, which brings awareness to and hopes to eradicate violence against Indigenous women, I recently hosted a self-defense class for women, in partnership with our local Brazilian Jiu Jitsu club. I followed it up with a class at the library called Yoga for Trauma, where we worked on reclaiming our bodies in a supportive and restorative environment.[20] I've included the poster and handout we made (figure 7.5), in case it inspires you to offer something similar in your own community. The most important thing I want you to take away from this is the significance of reaching out and making connections with people. Here in Canada we talk all the time about indigenizing our library spaces, making them more welcoming to our First Nation patrons, but it has to go beyond token gestures and move into genuine caring, inclusive policies, and

Danielle Shreve
and Lisa O'Donnell

Names: Danielle Shreve, Cataloger (left);

and Lisa O'Donnell, Adult Services Librarian (right)

Contacts: dshreve@stillwater.org; lodonnell@stillwater.org

Locations: Stillwater Public Library, Stillwater, Oklahoma

Claim to Fame: Healthy Literacy Series

All-Star Program: Tai Chi: Moving for Better Balance

Our Tai Chi program has been popular and successful because it encourages persons with any abilities to come and enjoy some movement and camaraderie in a relaxed atmosphere. We offer the instruction standing and sitting, encouraging movements that utilize as much of the body as the participant is able. The Stillwater Public Library started Tai Chi: Moving for Better Balance as part of our health literacy series and has continued it to enhance health literacy.

Tai Chi: Moving for Better Balance is an evidence-based fall prevention program that was designed to be used in community-based organizations. Accumulating evidence suggests that Tai Chi eight-form exercises are an effective means of improving balance, functional limitations, and muscle strength, which reduces the risk of falling. Tai Chi is a low-impact dance-like exercise that can be modified to meet the individual participant's needs and can be done in almost any location. It also helps build confidence from fear of falling, which is commonly found in older adults. The program is offered for adults of any ability. We encourage anyone to join and work to the best of their ability. We have also had success running a short introductory class to accommodate those with disabilities, utilizing props and games to keep it fun. Our upcoming fall introductory class will include information on stress and stress management. Graduates of all beginning tai chi classes are encouraged to join our continuing practice.

frontline program collaboration and collection development.[21] Libraries are *our* spaces: everyone's—this needs to be carried out in practice, not just in policy or good intentions.

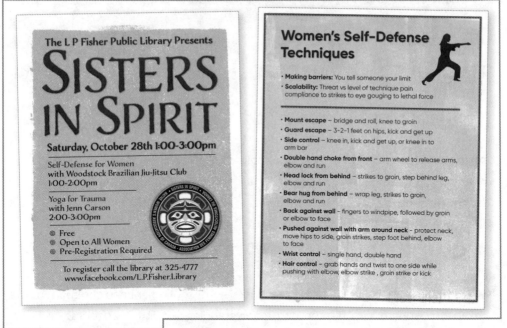

FIGURE 7.5 Sisters in Spirit poster; Self-Defense handout

Different Abilities

The first thing we need to do before we start planning on offering programs specifically for people with disabilities is to define what a "disability" is. Some people have physical, intellectual, or psychological variants that may create limitations or require adaptations, but these people aren't considered "disabled" under the social program model.[22] Even the government of Canada admits there is no common definition of "disability" in Canada, and in order to apply for social benefits, the person's condition (or combination of conditions) must be both severe (preventing them from working on a regular basis) and prolonged (indefinite and/or likely to result in death).[23] The U.S. Department of Labor takes the same approach.[24] So, in libraries, we have two reasonable approaches: create programs specifically designed for people with disabilities or that highlight the disabled, or work to adapt and integrate people of all abilities into existing programs.

If you've followed me this far, I think you can guess what sort of program model I prefer (though both types that I just mentioned have their place). For one thing, you avoid a possible public relations nightmare by making all programs inclusive and not calling attention to the disabilities of the attendees or presenters. I remember a recent thread on Facebook where a librarian was trying to host a storytime program with a person in a wheelchair as the presenter, and she was asking for advice about what to call the program.[25] She was thinking about calling it "Wheelchair Storytime." Some other suggestions were "Storytime on Wheels," "A Wheely Good Story Time," "Spoke and Word," and so on . . . which were all really cute, but the issue was: does highlighting the person's disability take away from the program, unnecessarily draw attention to their disability, or cause offense? Of the fifty-seven comments, there were many that were against the idea *totally* and thought it should just be called "Storytime." Period. One librarian who was a disability rights advocate weighed in and said that if the content of the storytime wasn't *about* having a disability, then it shouldn't be mentioned, unless by the presenter herself, or it ran the risk of being "inspirational porn."[26] The general consensus of most comments was that the presenter needed to be consulted first and that the program needed to be a collaboration. As one person summed it up, "Nothing about me, without me." I think this is the healthiest approach.

It is important to remember that not all disabilities will have an impact on performance, and you should never assume that you know someone's capabilities based on their diagnosis. If you've ever seen the film *Murderball* or watched the Paralympics, you already know that just because someone is severely disabled, this doesn't mean they aren't capable of high levels of physical performance, far beyond what those of us with typical bodies can achieve. Disability does not necessarily equal difficulty. Some of the children and teens I have taught with serious behavioral problems excelled at sports, where they could channel their extra energy and aggressive tendencies into something constructive and meaningful to them (unlike math homework, which they saw as irrelevant). Many adults in manual wheelchairs have much greater upper body

FIGURE 7.6 Chair yoga

strength than the general population because they are using their muscles so regularly for transportation. I am extremely myopic and have been since childhood, but I have excellent hearing and smelling abilities, no doubt developed to compensate for my lack of eyesight. If an activity or the equipment involved does get modified to suit someone's differentness, make sure the activity maintains its integrity and that the modifications aren't made as a token gesture to make it appear that we are being accommodating. The movement outcomes need to be evaluated on the basis of the task being performed, the resources the patron brings to the learning situation, and the context in which the activity takes place.[27] There is no room for being patronizing in authentic public service.

Library Staff—The Inreach

Let this statement sink in for a second: "The typical seated office worker *has more musculoskeletal injuries* than any other industry sector worker, including construction, metal industry, and transportation workers" (emphasis mine).[28] We have *more* injuries to our muscles and bones than people who build houses all day, *with power tools.* Some of the ramifications of sitting at a computer all day include neck pain, carpal tunnel syndrome, increased risk of heart disease, TMJ (jaw) disorder, pelvic floor dysfunction, weight gain, and tight hips, chest, and shoulders. I bet all of you know at least one of these conditions intimately (and I didn't even list them all). I know I do, and I work at a standing desk half the time and am physically active daily. As Kelly Starrett says in *Deskbound,* working out, even for more than an hour a day, isn't enough to counteract all of the negative repetitive strain and sedentary habits we regularly engage in, year after year. Our bodies are designed to be in motion, and when we are in motion to move fluidly, without pain and without causing injury. Exercise should therefore become a celebration of what our bodies are capable of, not a punishment for what we've eaten or a chore to huff our way through while staring at the television. Our bodies should be instruments of delight, tools we explore our environments with, not ornaments we are constantly trying to make prettier or jails we feel imprisoned in. But here I am, on my hypocritical high horse, with an able, mostly pain-free body, sitting at a desk, writing a book, while my shoulders tighten, my breath is shallow, and the blood pools in my legs and my toes go numb and my eyesight weakens.

TAKING CARE OF US
Advice for Library Staff

Feel like you are running full-throttle? Immobilized during downtime because there is just so much to catch up on? Exhausted and overwhelmed? Here are some tips that can help you take care of yourself:

SLEEP. The dishes can wait. **Everything looks better** after eight straight hours of shut-eye.

EAT FOOD that makes you feel good. Not too much of it. Eat it **mindfully**. Alone or with friends. You will be surprised by what (and how much) you put in your mouth when you really start paying attention to how it makes you feel.

DON'T BE RIGID. Rigidity is the enemy of fun. And I guarantee if you are reading this, **you need more fun.**

DO SOMETHING THAT SCARES YOU, in a good way. Just for you, **not to show off** or to post it on social media.

LAUGH. Don't take yourself too seriously. Or anyone else. Picture everyone who annoys you **wearing a clown nose** à la Bernie Glassman. Or to borrow from Elizabeth Lesser, remember we are all just "bozos on the bus."

MOVE YOUR BODY. A lot. You are less cranky when you walk on your lunch break, or go to the gym and lift weights, or run as hard as you can, or snowshoe with a friend, or play outdoors with your kids, or just use the stairs at work instead of the elevator. Even those of us with mobility issues can find ways **to be active**. Swimming and yoga are great low-impact activities.

MAKE ART. Colour. Dance. Grow things. Get your hands dirty. Play music. **With no agenda**, just because it feels good. Hug someone you love. Let yourself be helped when someone offers. Pet an animal.

BREATHE. When we're stressed or uncomfortable we tend to hold our breath or breathe shallowly. Take some deep, slow breaths. **Right now.** It can be helpful to put a reminder on your phone/desktop/watch every 30 minutes to remind you to breathe and to get up and move around.

RECONNECT with your spiritual or religious practice, whatever that may be. Try going for a walk in the woods and clearing your head. It can really help you **feel grounded** and connected. Or listen to some uplifting music with your eyes closed.

MORE ON THE WEB:
www.programminglibrarian.org
www.yogainthelibrary.com
www.physicalliteracyinthelibrary.com

Written and produced by Jenn Carson
Designed by Brendan Helmuth

FURTHER READING

The Art of Extreme Self Care by Cheryl Richardson. Especially the chapter "Let Me Disappoint You."

FIGURE 7.7 Taking Care of Us infographic

Last March I threw my back out and was off work, immobilized, for a week. Doctor's diagnosis? Too much sitting at my desk. The year before that, I had a recurring issue with my shoulder girdle. Diagnosis? Too much typing and mousing with that arm. Every time I go see the chiropractor, my neck gains about 30 percent more mobility. And I'm a yoga teacher—I stretch *all the time*. I can't imagine what the rest of your bodies feel like. Which is why I've made it my mandate to educate my fellow library colleagues on the importance of radical self-care. You can bet that at every staff meeting I attend, we do a stretch break. The "De-Stress Infographic" provided in chapter 5 was translated into French and distributed to everyone in the New Brunswick Public Library Service after the administration saw how effective it was. So I took it a step further and created another (figure 7.7).

I'm not the only library director who thinks staff self-care is no longer something to be considered a luxury; it's a necessity. Loriene Roy led the way, as we saw in this book's "Introduction," with the ALA's Wellness Initiatives a decade ago. In 2017, the Kokomo-Howard County Public Library in Indiana held a Summer Wellness Challenge, encouraging staff to try completing 10, 15, or 20 of the activities, with prizes to be won for participating.[29] To further help this idea along, I created a webinar for the ALA's Programming Librarian website in 2017.[30] And for when times at work get nearly unbearable, I wrote them a blog post called "Things Fall Apart: When Everything Goes Wrong" on how to cope at work and home when you just don't feel like you can manage anymore.[31] The feedback I got from librarians all over the continent made me realize just how many of us are hurting, how many people feel overwhelmed and under-supported, and how they were grateful to have the permission (not that they ever needed it, but for some reason they felt like they did) to *just take care of themselves.* Many of us are used to being "yes people": we're used to being the shoulder someone else cries on, the ones who have it all together, the ones who always have the answers or know where to find them, so it can be especially hard for us to admit, if not defeat, then difficulty. We have to learn that it is better to ask for help, to say the words out loud: "I am not coping very well right now." I'm here to tell you that it's okay that you are not okay right now. You will be. We're in this together.

Notes

1. Margaret Whitehead, "Motivation and the Significance of Physical Literacy in Every Individual," in *Physical Literacy throughout the Lifecourse,* ed. Margaret Whitehead (New York: Routledge, 2010), 32.
2. Download this at www.jenncarson.com/resources.html.
3. Personal correspondence with Aynslie Croney, used with permission.
4. Government of Canada, "Body Mass Index, Overweight or Obese, Self-Reported, by Age Group and Sex (Percent)," Statistics Canada, 2016, www.statcan.gc.ca/tables-tableaux/sum-som/101/cst01/health81b-eng.htm.

5. U.S. Department of Health and Human Services, "Overweight & Obesity Statistics," National Institute of Diabetes and Digestive and Kidney Diseases, 2017, https://www.niddk.nih.gov/health-information/health-statistics/overweight-obesity.

6. World Health Organization, "Controlling the Obesity Epidemic," Nutrition, 2003, www.who.int/nutrition/topics/obesity/en/.

7. Canadian Medical Association, "CMA Recognizes Obesity as a Disease," 2015, https://www.cma.ca/En/Pages/cma-recognizes-obesity-as-a-disease.aspx.

8. Paul Gately, "Physical Literacy and Obesity," in *Physical Literacy throughout the Lifecourse,* ed. Margaret Whitehead (New York: Routledge, 2010), 92.

9. W. H. Dietz, "Health Consequences of Obesity in Youth: Childhood Predictors of Adult Disease," *Pediatrics* 101 (March 1998): 518–25.

10. National Institute for Health and Care Excellence, "Obesity Prevention," 2015, https://www.nice.org.uk/guidance/cg43.

11. University of Vermont, "New Study: Exercise Reduces Suicide Attempts by Bullied Teens," University of Vermont: University News, 2015, www.uvm.edu/~uvmpr/?Page=news&storyID=21450.

12. Gately, "Physical Literacy and Obesity," 94.

13. Personal correspondence with author, September 12, 2017.

14. Follow the ALA's amazing Programming Librarian website to see what libraries all over North America are up to: www.programminglibrarian.org.

15. M. J. Rennie, "Anabolic Resistance: The Effects of Aging, Sexual Dimorphism, and Immobilization on Human Muscle Protein Turnover," *Applied Physiology, Nutrition and Metabolism* 3 (2009): 377–81.

16. Almond, "Physical Literacy and the Older Adult Population," in *Physical Literacy throughout the Lifecourse,* ed. Margaret Whitehead (New York: Routledge, 2010), 117.

17. Julia McKinnell, "Can You Get Fitter at 50 Than You've Ever Been in Your Life?" *Macleans,* 2014, www.macleans.ca/society/health/older-faster-and-way-stronger/?utm_source=Facebook&utm_medium=Promo&utm_campaign=macleans&utm_term=q3&utm_content=society.

18. To learn more about these programs, visit www.programminglibrarian.org/blog/one-community-celebrations-indigenous-history.

19. To learn more about this program, visit www.programminglibrarian.org/blog/childrens-programs-aboriginal-history-month.

20. To learn more about this program, please visit my blog post on the subject at the ALA's Programming Librarian website: http://www.programminglibrarian.org/user/25.

21. To see an example of how libraries are working to become more inclusive, check out the New Brunswick Public Library Service's policy for holding traditional smudging ceremonies: http://www2.gnb.ca/content/dam/gnb/Departments/nbpl-sbpnb/pdf/politiques-policies/1086_smudging.pdf.

22. Philip Vickerman and Karen DePauw, "Physical Literacy and Individuals with a Disability," in *Physical Literacy throughout the Lifecourse,* ed. Margaret Whitehead (New York: Routledge, 2010), 130.

23. Government of Canada, "Canada Pension Plan Disability Benefit—Overview," 2016, https://www.canada.ca/en/services/benefits/publicpensions/cpp/cpp-disability-benefit.html.

24. U.S. Department of Labor, "Frequently Asked Questions," Office of Disability Employment Policy, https://www.dol.gov/odep/faqs/general.htm.

25. If you belong to the group, you can access the thread here: https://www.facebook.com/groups/ALAthinkTANK/search/?query=wheelchair%20storytime.

26. Catherine Soper, "How to Avoid 'Inspiration Porn' When Talking about Disability," The Mighty, 2016, https://themighty.com/2016/08/how-to-avoid-inspiration-porn-when-talking-about-disability/.

27. Vickerman and DePauw, "Physical Literacy and Individuals with a Disability," 133–34.

28. Kelly Starrett, Juliet Starrett, and Glen Cordoza, *Deskbound: Standing Up to a Sitting World* (Las Vegas, NV: Victory Belt, 2016).

29. Faith Brautigam, "Summer Wellness Challenge," Public Libraries Online, 2017, http://publiclibrariesonline.org/2017/08/summer-wellness-challenge/.

30. Check it out at www.programminglibrarian.org/learn/taking-care-us-ergonomic-advice-library-staff.

31. Check it out at www.programminglibrarian.org/blog/things-fall-apart-when-everything-goes-wrong.

Creating the Spaces They Deserve

Providing Opportunities for Whole-Person Literacy in Our Communities

> . . . Let me
> keep my mind on what matters,
> which is my work,
> which is mostly standing still and learning to be
> astonished.
>
> —*Mary Oliver*

While I am rarely, if ever, standing still like Mary Oliver, I completely empathize with having one's life's work consist of "learning to be astonished." Every time I intuit roadblocks ahead, or worry that no one will show up for a program, or fear there won't be enough funding, space, time, or energy to accomplish the task at hand, I take a deep breath and listen to the people all around me—who have their own fears, time constraints, responsibilities, and physical limitations—shouting an enthusiastic "Yes!" Sometimes, on the hard days, it's only me quietly whispering it to myself. I look up at the trees for inspiration, as Mother Nature turns the seasons and pushes on through the chaos and maintains the rhythm of our days. Somehow, someway, everything gets done, exactly when it is supposed to.

While writing this book, I went back and looked over my old notebooks from the beginning of this journey into discovering what it meant to have a body, and how changing your body could also mean changing your mind. For years it seemed like I lived almost entirely in my head. As an academic, a poet, an artist, and a thinker, I valued myself cerebrally, but my body felt more like an unreliable vehicle I used (and barely knew how to drive) to get my head where it needed to go. After my first son was born in 2007, I suffered from some pretty crippling postpartum obsessive-compulsive symptoms, and one of the things that saved me (besides the love and patience of my family and friends—and therapy/medication) was yoga. In fact, I have often said that it was *the* major contributing factor to my healing. It contributed not just to my surviving, but to my actually thriving and never going back to that dark place again, even after subsequent births and other much worse traumas and stressors. And it wasn't just the movement and breathing exercises that brought me back to health; it was the shared experience with others, the community of souls all showing up, ready to suffer and laugh together. This inspired me to pursue my yoga teacher training, first with kids and then with adults. This inspired me to get out of my head and into my heart and my body, and then eventually to give back by connecting with others. Getting physical, and really paying attention to my breath and body, allowed me to take control over my super-active imagination and use it creatively, for good, instead of self-destructively, where it would turn into anxiety and catastrophizing. I started thinking that maybe I wasn't the only one going through this. Maybe there was a subset of the population who were going through the motions of living but inside were in deep emotional crisis—they were disconnected from the people they needed the most, and they lacked the tools to bring themselves into healthy coherence with the natural world. In fact, the more I really listened to others as they told me their stories, I thought maybe this subgroup included most of us.

Reading through my old notes, I came across this passage I wrote in my journal a few days before Christmas in 2010, my first semester into managing the library at Hampton High School:

> The "work" of childhood is the development, exploration, and refinement of the imagination. This is achieved through play, which can be modeled by adults, or at least initiated. So many children are now entertained or kept busy through soccer "practice" (don't you actually learn how to handle a soccer ball by just playing with it?); through dance "lessons" (what happened to just dancing to old records with your parents for fun?); through television and toys that are either marketed through television or developed as marketing tools for a television show—toys with scripts children are expected to follow. At the high school, I'm watching an entire generation of kids that are apathetic to almost everything that involves physical effort or their own imaginative input.

> Isn't curiosity the hallmark of childhood and adolescence? Why is it becoming extinct? How do we save it? An active imagination and a rich inner world are essential for thriving in (not just surviving) the (sometimes) drudgery of adulthood.

I wrote this only a few weeks after I had started the Hampton High Library Guild—my far-out attempt to get some isolated teens more involved, enthused, and connected with each other; and an effort to create something we could all care about that was greater than ourselves—a community. But that idea, like all the programming ideas in this book, grew out of seeds that had been planted many years before.

It wasn't like one day I just woke up and realized that moving my body and being aware of its shifting states (physical literacy) were deeply interrelated with other essential literacies like thinking clearly, writing articulately, managing my finances, speaking effectively, listening with an open heart, navigating the Web, organizing my time productively, being competent in social interactions, and feeling in control of my emotions. After working so hard to heal all these (what felt like) disparate parts of myself and then watching the children, teens, and adults I worked with begin to integrate their various skills and find their lives more in balance, it dawned on me that there was a natural gestalt, a place of wholeness that is more than just the sum of its parts. I saw that when people lived and loved from this place of integration, they were naturally healthy, and healthy people were compelled to support and even raise the health of everyone around them, not just by being a role model, but because they were genuinely overjoyed when other people thrived. Good living is not a pie that only has enough pieces for a few, select individuals—those who perhaps won life's lottery by being given able bodies, straight teeth, overflowing trust funds, balanced brain chemistry, and perfect eyesight. Knowing how to live a healthy life—having whole-person literacy—is the right of every single person on this planet, regardless of the circumstances they were born into or that arose around them. And it dawned on me that librarians, who are already wearing so many other hats—social worker, career coach, tech specialist, health advisor, tourism coordinator, tax consultant, teacher, editor, event coordinator, marketing guru, networking pro, and occasionally nonviolent interventionist—are in a perfect position to be able to address many of the overlapping (and sometimes conflicting) needs of their patrons. In fact, we are

FIGURE C.1 Mini-golf

already doing it (see figure C.1). And libraries, especially public libraries, are already in a position to provide many of these services, as we have moved away from focusing solely on providing textual and auditory information services and are becoming true community centers focusing on the wellness of everyone—of all ages, cultural backgrounds, socioeconomic status, levels of health, abilities, or genders. And we provide it for free. No other institution on this planet, government-funded or otherwise, offers such an all-encompassing slew of services, and no one but librarians and library staff have the skills, patience, creativity, experience, and grit to do it. We are a special tribe, operating out of a remarkable, revolutionary tradition.

My sincerest hope is that you will take this book and the program ideas inside it and go into your library, your community, and do what you are already doing—being awesome—but do it armed with a just few more tools, a bit more theory to give you confidence, some data so you have scientific proof you are making a difference, and all the enthusiasm you can muster—to plan, promote, and deliver compelling physical literacy programs to your patrons (and staff). And I hope that you will have fun while doing it. I'm proud of you for everything you have already accomplished. Now get out there—and play!

Broadening Our Concept of "Literacy" to Include Physical Literacy

Dr. Denise Agosto

For many decades, public librarians across the United States have been working hard to deliver library programs that promote the healthy cognitive and social development of their community members. These programs tend to be tied to traditional as well as newer conceptions of literacy, such as summer reading programs, author talks, technology skills lessons, film and other media presentations, and more. Although public library programs designed to encourage healthy physical development are on the rise, they still represent a small minority of library program offerings. It's time now for public libraries to offer greater numbers of programs designed to support the healthy physical development of their community members, and to move toward thinking of physical literacy as one of the crucial components of literacy in general.

Why should encouraging physical health be the purview of public libraries, institutions that were originally created to promote books and traditional literacy? The answer to this question lies in the core mission of today's public library writ large. The role of any public library is to serve the needs of its community, and most U.S. communities are in desperate need of more physical activity outlets. Most American adults get significantly less than recommended amounts of physical activity, and the majority of American parents are concerned with the lack of physical education in their children's schools (Harvard School of Public Health 2013). In fact, less than 5 percent of American adults participate in at least thirty minutes of physical activity each day (U.S. Department of Agriculture 2010), and just one-third of American adults average at least the minimum recommended amounts of physical activity each week (U.S. Department of Health and Human Services 2010). The situation is no better among America's children; less than one-quarter of children meet the recommended physical activity guidelines (SHAPE America 2016).

These statistics are alarming, but public libraries are well-positioned to play a significant role in addressing this widespread lack of physical activity among their community members. The vision of public libraries as "centers for wellness," laid out in the first chapter of this book, shows how public libraries can work toward providing badly needed physical activity and physical education opportunities in their communities.

In addition to fulfilling pressing community needs, providing programs and services aimed at increasing community physical health can (and should) also be viewed as part of the literacy mission of the public library. The breadth of the definition of "literacy" is ever-expanding, and the range of library programs and services aimed at supporting community literacy is expanding in turn. To this point, in June 2016 I delivered a speech at the Tenth International Symposium on Library Services for Children and Young Adults in Seoul, South Korea (Agosto 2016). In that speech I identified six trends in public library services for teens. Even though I focused on youth audiences, these trends extend to adult audiences as well. One of the six trends was "a broadening of literacy and learning goals beyond reading" (32). This means that public libraries are working to create programs and services designed to support user literacy in a wider range of new and emerging information environments than ever before.

In other words, "literacy" in today's multifarious information environments means much more than just the ability to read and write well enough to function in everyday society (commonly referred to as "functional literacy"). The professional literature is peppered with new labels for new types of literacy that encompass a wide and growing range of skills and knowledge. Some of the more popular terms include "digital literacy" (the ability to use information technology effectively), "media literacy" (which includes both technology know-how and the ability to read, create, and evaluate information in a variety of formats), "critical literacy" (having the skills and knowledge necessary for effective participation in democratic society), and "transliteracy (the ability to read, write, and create information across a range of different media platforms). Of course, the term "information literacy" (the ability to access, evaluate, and use information effectively) remains highly popular in the library literature as well.

The point here is not that any one of these terms is "correct," but that as a field, we are moving toward a broader definition of "literacy." When I first identified this trend while writing my 2016 speech, I must admit that I didn't think to include physical literacy within the newer, broadened conception of literacy. Instead, I focused on new media platforms and the skills needed for the effective use of these new media, rather than focusing on expanding the definition to additional human developmental areas beyond just cognitive and social development, which had previously been most commonly associated with the concept of literacy.

Get Your Community Moving: Physical Literacy Programs for All Ages has served as a wake-up call for me personally because it points out clearly that *physical literacy is literacy,* and as such, library programs that promote physical movement and physical education should be viewed as a part of the core mission of the modern public library. Indeed, this book should serve as an important call to all of us in the public library field to remember that humans are as much physical beings as we are social, emotional, and cognitive beings, and that for public libraries to serve their community members' full range of literacy needs, we must offer movement-based programs in addition to more traditional literacy programs that revolve around reading, writing, media literacy, digital literacy, and so on.

Of course, movement-based programs and more traditional information literacy-based programs should by no means be thought of as mutually exclusive. As the model library programs outlined in this volume show, programs that encourage physical movement can be combined with traditional reading- and writing-based literacy programs, with digital skills programs, with visual and artistic literacy programs, and more. The opportunities for creating new library programs to serve the whole person in the community are endless as long as we remember that humans are not just thinking and feeling beings but physical beings as well. Physical literacy *is* literacy.

References

Agosto, D. E. 2016, September. "'Hey! The Library Is Kind of Awesome!' Current Trends in U.S. Public Library Services for Teens." *Public Libraries* 55: 30–34, 39.

Harvard School of Public Health. 2013, September. "Education and Health in Schools: A Survey of Parents." https://www.rwjf.org/content/dam/farm/reports/surveys_and_polls/2013/rwjf407960.

SHAPE America. 2016. "Report: Less Than One Quarter of Children in the U.S. Meet Current Physical Activity Guidelines." www.shapeamerica.org/pressroom/2016/2016-us-report-card-on-physical -activity.cfm.

U.S. Department of Agriculture. "Dietary Guidelines for Americans, 2010." www.cnpp.usda.gov/ dietaryguidelines.htm.

U.S. Department of Health and Human Services. "Healthy People 2010." www.cdc.gov/nchs/healthy_people/ hp2010.htm.

Movement-Based Holidays

January
JANUARY 3 National Fruitcake Toss Day (USA)

Second Wednesday in January: National Take the Stairs Day (USA)

JANUARY 17 International Kid Inventors Day

JANUARY 18 World Snowman Day

February
FEBRUARY 8 National Kite Flying Day (USA)

FEBRUARY 23 National Play Tennis Day (USA)

March
Nutrition Month (USA, CAN)

First Friday in March: National Day of Unplugging (USA)

MARCH 3 World Wildlife Day

MARCH 5 World Tennis Day

MARCH 10 National Pack Your Lunch Day (USA)

MARCH 12 National Plant a Flower Day (USA)

MARCH 18 World Sleep Day

MARCH 20 International Happiness Day

MARCH 20 World Storytelling Day

MARCH 21 World Puppetry Day

MARCH 22 World Water Day

MARCH 30 National Take a Walk in the Park Day (USA)

April
First Wednesday in April: National Walking Day (USA)

First Friday in April: National Walk to Work Day (USA)

First Full Week of April: National Public Health Week (USA)

APRIL 3 World Party Day

APRIL 3 National Find a Rainbow Day (USA)

APRIL 4 National Walk around Things Day (USA)

APRIL 6 National Student-Athlete Day (USA)

APRIL 7 World Health Day

APRIL 22 Earth Day

APRIL 23 National Picnic Day (USA)

APRIL 29 International Dance Day

Last Full Week of April: National Medical Fitness Week (USA)

Last Full Week of April: Every Kid Healthy Week (USA)

May

National Bike Month (USA, CAN)

National Golf Month (USA, CAN)

First Saturday in May: World Naked Gardening Day

MAY 4 National Weather Observer's Day (USA)

MAY 11 National Foam Rolling Day (USA)

Second Saturday in May: National Archery Day (USA)

Second Saturday in May: National Miniature Golf Day (USA)

MAY 14 Dance like a Chicken Day (USA)

MAY 16 National Love a Tree Day (USA)

Third Thursday in May: Global Accessibility Awareness Day

Third Friday in May: National Bike to Work Day (USA, CAN)

Third Saturday in May: National Learn to Swim Day (USA)

Third Sunday in May: National Take Your Parents to a Playground Day (USA)

MAY 24 National Scavenger Hunt Day (USA)

MAY 25 National Tap Dance Day (USA)

Last Wednesday in May: National Senior Health and Fitness Day (USA)

June

First Full Week of June: National Gardening Week (USA)

Men's Health Week (always ends on Father's Day)

First Wednesday in June: National Running Day (USA)

First Saturday in June: National Health and Fitness Day (CAN)

JUNE 6 National Yo-Yo Day (USA)

JUNE 6 National Gardening Exercise Day (USA)

JUNE 13 National Weed Your Garden Day (USA)

JUNE 15 National Nature Photography Day (USA/CAN)

JUNE 17 World Juggling Day

JUNE 18 International Picnic Day

JUNE 20 International Surfing Day

JUNE 21 World Music Day

JUNE 21 International Yoga Day

JUNE 21 National Go Skateboarding Day (USA)

July

Last Saturday in July: National Dance Day (USA)

JULY 31 International Uncommon Musical Instrument Day

August

National Golf Month (USA)

National Family Fun Month (USA)

First Saturday in August: National Disc Golf Day (USA)

AUGUST 2 National Coloring Book Day (USA/CAN)

AUGUST 6 National Wiggle Your Toes Day (USA)

AUGUST 8 National Bowling Day (USA/CAN)

Second Saturday in August: National Bowling Day (USA)

AUGUST 27 National Tug-of-War Day (USA)

September

National Self-Improvement Month (USA)

National Yoga Month (USA)

SEPTEMBER 8 World Physical Therapy Day

SEPTEMBER 8 World Literacy Day

SEPTEMBER 12 World Video Game Day

SEPTEMBER 16 International Coastal Clean-Up Day

Third Saturday in September: National Gymnastics Day (USA)

Last Wednesday in September: National Women's Health and Fitness Day (USA)

Last Saturday in September: National Family Health and Fitness Day (USA)

October

Health Literacy Month

International Walk to School Month

OCTOBER 2 National Child Health Day (USA)

First Wednesday in October: National Walk to School Day (USA)

First Full Week of October: National Spinning and Weaving Week (USA)

OCTOBER 8 American Touch Tag Day

OCTOBER 25 International Artists Day

November

NOVEMBER 15 I Love to Write Day (USA)

NOVEMBER 17 National Take a Hike Day (USA)

NOVEMBER 20 National Child Day (CAN)

NOVEMBER 29 National Square Dancing Day (USA)

December

DECEMBER 3 International Day of Persons with Disabilities

DECEMBER 28 National Card Playing Day (USA)

GLOSSARY OF TERMS

Body Language: Nonverbal messages that are communicated through movements, facial expressions, and voice tone and volume.

Diaphragm: Large muscle that extends across the bottom of the thoracic cavity, separating it from the abdominal cavity below. It is essential for respiration; as it contracts, air is drawn into the lungs.

Fight-or-Flight Response: Also known as the "stress response" to a *perceived* threat to survival. It occurs when the adrenal glands secrete the hormone adrenaline, which increases heart rate and arouses the sympathetic nervous system while reducing activity in the parasympathetic nervous system. The response makes us feel like we want to attack ("fight") whatever has triggered us, or run away ("flight").

Fine Motor Skills: Small movements of the wrists, hands, and fingers in coordination with the eyes (such as holding a pencil or sewing).

Gross Motor Skills: Large movements carried out by the body repeatedly with accuracy and precision (such as running, jumping, crawling).

Inner Core: A group of muscles that stabilize the spine and pelvis, including the transverse abdominus, multifidi, diaphragm, and pelvic floor.

Midline: Center of the body that divides it into right and left halves.

Mirror Neuron: A neuron that fires when an action is planned, acted, or observed, thereby mentally mirroring another's behavior.

Multifidus (pl. multifidi): Small muscle that runs along the spine, connecting segments of vertebrae together.

Muscle Memory: When a movement is repeated over time, a long-term muscle memory is created neurologically, so that eventually the movement can be performed without conscious effort.

Myopia: Nearsightedness. The inability to see things far away.

Outer Core: Large stability muscles that produce force and move the body.

Pelvic Floor: A group of muscles deep in the pelvis that support the bladder, bowel, and (in women) the uterus.

Physical Literacy: Also known as 'bodily-kinesthetic intelligence," it is the motivation, ability, confidence, and understanding to move the body throughout the life course as is appropriate to each person's given endowment.

Postural Control: The ability to maintain body alignment.

Proprioception: The ability to sense, without seeing, where one's body parts are in relation to each other and the surrounding environment.

Self-Regulate: The ability to be in control of one's emotions.

Sensory Disorganization: A state that occurs when too many senses are being activated at once and one becomes overwhelmed with sensory data.

Sensory Integration: The act of processing, organizing, and understanding incoming data for functional use.

Synesthetic Perception: Perception that occurs when our external sense receptors (i.e., eyes and ears) and our internal sense receptors (i.e., proprioception) work together to give us a holistic understanding of our environment and the objects in it.

Tacit Knowledge: A knowledge that is difficult to acquire through traditional written or verbal information transfer. A skill that often is acquired through a combination of formal training, psychological makeup, and experience. For example, leadership or reading body language.

Tactile Defensiveness: An adversity and hypersensitivity to touch and coming into contact with everyday objects such as sand, grass, dirt, or clothing seams and tags.

Theory of Mind: The ability to attribute different mind states to oneself and others, and to understand that people can have perceptions and beliefs that differ from one's own.

Transverse Abdominus: Deep muscle that wraps around your spine, connecting the lower ribs to the hips, creating stability.

Utricles: The fluid-filled cavity of the inner ear that contains hair cells and otoliths and sends messages to the brain about the orientation of the head.

Vestibular System: Bodily system that controls motion, balance, and spatial orientation; it allows one to navigate the environment with ease and grace.

BIBLIOGRAPHY

Abram, Stephen. "Librarian Hobbies!! Here Are the Results." Stephen's Lighthouse: Illuminating Library Industry Trends, Innovation, and Information. 2010. http://stephenslighthouse.com/2010/10/31/librarian-hobbies-here-are-the-results/.

Active for Life. "Active for Life: Raising Physically Literate Kids." 2017. http://activeforlife.com/.

Almond, Len. "Physical Literacy and the Older Adult Population." In *Physical Literacy throughout the Lifecourse*, edited by Margaret Whitehead, 116–29. New York: Routledge, 2010.

Anji Play World. "True Play: A Movement of Children, Teachers, Families, and Communities." Anji Play. 2017. www.anjiplay.com/home/#trueplay.

Ayres, Ed. *The Longest Race: A Lifelong Runner, an Iconic Ultramarathon, and the Case for Human Endurance*. New York: Experiment, 2012.

Bachynsky, Ivan, and Jennifer Bachynsky. OT Kids Can. 2017. http://otkidscan.com/.

Bertot, J. C., et al. "2014 Digital Inclusion Survey: Survey Findings and Results." University of Maryland, College Park: Information Policy and Access Center (iPAC), 2015. http://digitalinclusion.umd.edu/sites/default/files/uploads/2014DigitalInclusionSurveyFinalRelease.pdf.

Canadian Medical Association. "CMA Recognizes Obesity as a Disease." 2015. https://www.cma.ca/En/Pages/cma-recognizes-obesity-as-a-disease.aspx.

Canadian Sport Tourism Alliance. "Sport Tourism Surges Past $6.5 Billion Annually." Canadian Sport Tourism Alliance News. 2017. http://canadiansporttourism.com/news/sport-tourism-surges-past-65-billion-annually.html.

Carson, Jenn. "Physical Literacy: Movement-Based Programs in Libraries." Survey. 2017. https://docs.google.com/forms/d/1q9L5uwuk6QQSug8afUp5dT51FM5NVU1_5j_-PoxRWis/edit?usp=sharing_eil&ts=59b284ff.

——. Programming Librarian. Blog. 2015-present. www.programminglibrarian.org/users/jcarson.

Connell, Gill, and Cheryl McCarthy. *A Moving Child Is a Learning Child: How the Body Teaches the Brain to Think*. Grand Valley, MN: Free Spirit, 2014.

Dietz, W. H. "Health Consequences of Obesity in Youth: Childhood Predictors of Adult Disease." *Pediatrics* 101 (March 1998): 518–25.

Dunn, Rita, Kenneth Dunn, and Janet Perrin. *Teaching Young Children through Their Individual Learning Styles: Practical Approaches for Grades K-2*. Toronto, ON: Pearson, 1994.

EA Games/Electronic Arts. *Harry Potter Quidditch World Cup*. Redwood City, CA: EA Games/Electronic Arts, 2005.

Fox, Kenneth. "The Physical Self and Physical Literacy." In *Physical Literacy throughout the Lifecourse*, edited by Margaret Whitehead, 71–82. New York: Routledge, 2010.

Gately, Paul. "Physical Literacy and Obesity." In *Physical Literacy throughout the Lifecourse*, edited by Margaret Whitehead, 83–99. New York: Routledge, 2010.

Gladwell, Malcolm. *Blink: The Power of Thinking without Thinking*. New York: Little, Brown, 2005.

GoNoodle. "GoNoodle." https://www.gonoodle.com/.

Government of Canada. "Body Mass Index, Overweight or Obese, Self-Reported, by Age Group and Sex (Percent)." Statistics Canada. 2016. www.statcan.gc.ca/tables-tableaux/sum-som/101/cst01/health81b-eng.htm.

——. "Canada's Law on Spam and Other Electronic Threats." Canada's Anti-Spam Legislation. 2017. http://fightspam.gc.ca/eic/site/030.nsf/eng/home.

_____ . "Canada Pension Plan Disability Benefit—Overview." 2016. https://www.canada.ca/en/services/benefits/publicpensions/cpp/cpp-disability-benefit.html.

Gray, Peter. "How to Ruin Children's Play: Supervise, Praise, Intervene." _Psychology Today._ 2009. https://www.psychologytoday.com/blog/freedom-learn/200901/how-ruin-children-s-play-supervise-praise-intervene.

Hannaford, Carla. _Playing in the Unified Field: Raising & Becoming Conscious, Creative Human Beings._ Salt Lake City, UT: Great River Books, 2010.

_____ . _Smart Moves: Why Learning Is Not All in Your Head._ Salt Lake City, UT: Great River Books, 2005.

Hanscom, Angela J. _Balanced and Barefoot: How Unrestricted Outdoor Play Makes for Strong, Confident, and Capable Children._ Oakland, CA: New Harbinger, 2016.

HHS Library Guild. "HHS Library Guild: Where the Geek Will Inherit the Earth." 2011. http://hhslibraryguild.blogspot.ca/.

International Physical Literacy Association. "Physical Literacy." 2016. https://www.physical-literacy.org.uk/.

International Play Association. "Declaration on the Importance of Play." IPA World. 2014. http://ipaworld.org/wp-content/uploads/2015/05/IPA_Declaration-FINAL.pdf.

Kellogg-Hubbard Library. "StoryWalk." 2012. www.kellogghubbard.org/storywalk.

Kwar, Mary J., and Ron Frick. _Astronaut Training: A Sound-Activated Vestibular-Visual Protocol for Moving, Looking, and Listening._ Madison, WI: Vital Links, 2005.

Lenstra, Noah. "Let's Move in Libraries." Let's Move in Libraries. 2017. www.LetsMoveLibraries.org/.

Living Works Education. "ASIST Two-Day Training." 2016. https://www.livingworks.net/programs/asist/.

MacKenzie, Kevin. "Fingerplays!" Stories by Kevin. www.storiesbykevin.com/fingersplay.html.

Maude, Patricia. "Physical Literacy and the Young Child." In _Physical Literacy throughout the Lifecourse,_ edited by Margaret Whitehead, 100–115. New York: Routledge, 2010.

National Association of Sports Commissions. "National Association of Sports Commissions Releases Annual State of the Industry Report." 2017. https://www.sportscommissions.org/Blog/article/ID/738/National-Association-of-Sports-Commissions-Releases-Annual-State-of-the-Industry-Report.

National Institute for Health and Care Excellence. "Obesity Prevention." 2015. https://www.nice.org.uk/guidance/cg43.

Pang, Alex Soojung-Kim. _Rest: Why You Get More Done When You Work Less._ New York: Basic Books, 2016.

Pearce, Joseph Chilton. _Magical Child._ New York: Plume, 1992.

Programming Librarian. "Taking Care of Us: Ergonomic Advice for Library Staff." YouTube. 2017. https://www.youtube.com/watch?v=E_HBGZVglv0.

Ratey, J. J., and E. Hagerman. _SPARK: The Revolutionary New Science of Exercise and the Brain._ New York: Little, Brown, 2008.

Rennie, M. J. "Anabolic Resistance: The Effects of Aging, Sexual Dimorphism, and Immobilization on Human Muscle Protein Turnover." _Applied Physiology, Nutrition and Metabolism_ 3 (2009): 377–81.

Rouleau, Natasha, and Josée Leblanc. "ABC Boum!" http://abcboum.net/.

Rowling, J. K., and Tomislav Tomic. _Quidditch through the Ages._ London: Bloomsbury, 2017.

Scherrer, Katie. _Stories, Songs, and Stretches! Creating Playful Storytimes with Yoga and Movement._ Chicago: American Library Association, 2017.

SOCAN. "Licensing FAQs." 2012. https://www.socan.ca/licensees/faq-licensing.

Starrett, Kelly, Juliet Starrett, and Glen Cordoza. _Deskbound: Standing Up to a Sitting World._ Las Vegas, NV: Victory Belt, 2016.

Superhero N. B. "Superhero Training." https://www.superhero-nb.ca/.

Thomas, Lee. "Together We Can Break the Silence." https://www.leethomas.ca/.

Timbernook. "Innovative Nature-Based Programming." Timbernook: The Ultimate Sensory Experience. 2017. www.timbernook.com/2017/index.html.

Trehearne, Miriam P. *Multiple Paths to Literacy: Proven High-Yield Strategies to Scaffold Emerging Literacy Learning across the Curriculum.* Calgary, AB: Miriam P. Trehearne Literacy Consulting, 2016.

University of Vermont. "New Study: Exercise Reduces Suicide Attempts by Bullied Teens." University of Vermont: University News. 2015. www.uvm.edu/~uvmpr/?Page=news&storyID=21450.

U.S. Department of Health and Human Services. "Overweight & Obesity Statistics." National Institute of Diabetes and Digestive and Kidney Diseases. 2017. https://www.niddk.nih.gov/health-information/health-statistics/overweight-obesity.

U.S. Department of Labor. "Frequently Asked Questions." Office of Disability Employment Policy. https://www.dol.gov/odep/faqs/general.htm.

Vickerman, Philip, and Karen DePauw. "Physical Literacy and Individuals with a Disability." In *Physical Literacy throughout the Lifecourse,* edited by Margaret Whitehead, 130–41. New York: Routledge, 2010.

Whitehead, Margaret. "The Concept of Physical Literacy." In *Physical Literacy throughout the Lifecourse,* edited by Margaret Whitehead, 10–20. New York: Routledge, 2010.

———. "Introduction." In *Physical Literacy throughout the Lifecourse,* edited by Margaret Whitehead, 3–9. New York: Routledge, 2010.

———. "Motivation and the Significance of Physical Literacy for Every Individual." In *Physical Literacy throughout the Lifecourse,* edited by Margaret Whitehead, 30–43. New York: Routledge, 2010.

World Health Organization. "Controlling the Obesity Epidemic." Nutrition. 2003. www.who.int/nutrition/topics/obesity/en/.

INDEX